TRAINS AND
RAILWAYS
OF AUSTRALIA

TRAINS AND RAILWAYS OF AUSTRALIA

JIM POWE

NEW
HOLLAND

CONTENTS

When I was four years old it was 1939 and war was about to be declared. My family lived in the Melbourne suburb of Sandringham. It was a corner house on Bluff Road. I recall four silver lines buried in the road that curved as they turned the corner into Royal Avenue.

The Sandringham Tram at Black Rock, 1955.

Every fortnight my family and I would catch this strange vehicle called a tram. It made use of two of those curving lines I was so curious about. As a youngster, I thought a tram was a strange beast—it made such a distinctive noise as it rolled along the street. Above the tram was a long pole with a wheel on the end pressed up against an overhead wire. As we travelled, the vehicle would screech around the curves, while along the straights the pole would create a twanging sound on the overhead wire.

The tram would take us to Sandringham Railway Station. Later I would find out that the tram line was operated by Victorian Railways. This isolated tram line closed in 1956 and was standard gauge, as is the main Melbourne tramway system.

At Sandringham we would board the waiting train. Some electric train carriages had compartments that were entered by a single door off the platform. I learnt much later they were suburban carriages once hauled by steam engines. Off we went to Melbourne and I can still hear the whining of the gears, particularly when I sat over the motor bogie. I could hear when the driver applied power—or cut the power off to coast, as the gear noise would change.

I remember passing Brighton Railway Station with its short dead-end curved platform, which in those days was for special trains from Melbourne to Brighton Beach.

I recall the smell of tomatoes as we passed the Rosella Tomato Sauce factory beside the line and the excitement of passing sidings with electric trains stabled in them. These, of course, were there to begin the peak afternoon services.

The train pulled into Flinders Street Railway Station where we alighted. Typically, we would have a meat pie and firm jellies at the old Coles cafeteria, just down the street from the station.

One weekend, Dad took the family into Flinders Street, but onto another, very long platform compared to the normal one. A very different train stood at the platform. On the front, as I later learnt, was a steam locomotive. Dad lifted me up onto the running board next to the steam engine's boiler. He held me and I could feel the warmth coming off this massive object. It was hissing gently—just like a kettle.

ABOVE Port Melbourne and the Railway Pier in the mid 1880s, replaced by Station Pier in the 1920s.

It scared me. I started to scream and yell. As Dad lifted me back down off the engine, I happened to turn around and saw the fireman on his seat in the engine's cabin grinning at me through his window. I am quite sure that this humiliation psychologically affected me for the rest of my life!

We moved away from the engine and boarded the train. It was at this point that I heard the roar of the engine's whistle and we started off with a very unusual chuffing noise. We were off for a day trip to Geelong.

Somewhere along the way I went out into the carriage corridor, kneeling so that my forearms were on the window sill, with the window raised. I knelt there gazing to the west where I could see a grey blue mountain range in the distance. They were the granite You Yangs. I wondered what was over those mountains.

I believe this was the beginning of my lifelong interest in travelling and wondering what lay beyond...

Much later my railway colleagues told me that I journeyed on a train hauled by an A2 locomotive that day—*The Flyer*.

Another time Dad took our landlady and me in her car to Melbourne's Station Pier. I remember driving onto the pier and being fascinated by the railway lines lying there between the timbers of the pier decking. To the west I could see the side of a huge ship onto which baggage was being lifted in giant cargo nets. Our landlady was off onto a south sea cruise. Before long, my attention was drawn by the demanding whistle of a steam engine; and there approaching was the Boat Train from the city.

My ageing memory tells me that the engine, if not the whole train, was painted blue. It was a marvellous sight—and one that is indelibley etched in my mind.

Not long after I remember making the journey to Sydney. I was travelling with the family and we boarded *Spirit of Progress* on Number 1 platform at Spencer Street. What a sight it was—royal blue with gold striping, shiny and with a resplendid 'S' class locomotive up the front. She was adorned with golden wings near the headlight and her art deco styling told me she was the pride of the railways.

We were fortunate to have made this journey. War had just broken out, and it was very difficult to get accommodation on the train. Dad took me forward on the speeding train at night. I remember reaching the baggage van at the front. I could hear the racing exhaust going at over 70 miles per hour (112 km/h) on this amazing engine, which had the largest driving wheels in Australia.

We stood near the open door. There was a bar across it. I remember Dad holding me as we listened to the roar of the engine. Outside in the dark I saw, in a flash, a circle of men

Wig wag crossing
PHOTO: RTBU NSW

sitting around a blazing fire. For many, life was lived beside these open campfires. The Depression so many years before was still taking its toll and work was not always easy to come by. These men collected coal from the railway lines where it had fallen from locomotive tenders—and was shovelled onto the track by compassionate firemen for these luckless souls.

I was getting tired by the time the *Spirit* terminated at Albury. Dad lifted me onto his shoulders to reveal a huge throng of milling people. These people were making their way to the two New South Wales trains—one behind the other—on the long platform. The train in the lead was the *Melbourne Limted Express* while behind the *Melbourne Express* waited, with mostly sitting cars.

We boarded the rear train and found a second class compartment. Both trains were hauled by 36 class locomotives. I remember waking on my mother's lap with the train puffing along well into NSW, heading to Sydney. Gazing out the window I could see the engine curving with the train through green fields. There was a clump of trees near the top of a hill with the clouds seemingly rising out of them.

I called to Mum: 'Look there's a cloud being born!'

We alighted at Strathfield and made our way to a different platform where we caught a much smarter looking electric train to Parramatta....the place where I was to grow up. As we left Parramatta station, I recall being fascinated by the steam engine shunting in the goods yard on the north side. We were home.

Parramatta was alive with steam—and it wasn't always on the main railway. I remember having my hair cut in George Street, and being delighted by the sound of a whistle...it was the steam tram crossing Church Street. The tram was part of life in Parramatta, carrying linseed and other goods to and from Meggitts Mill until the 1940s. I recall the conductor with his stock whip, keeping the pesky schoolchildren in line as they tried to board the moving toast rack carriage.

On occasion we all went to visit an uncle at Camden. This began with a ride in an electric train from Parramatta Station, changing to a steam train that carried us to Campbelltown. Here we alighted and I remember watching the train travelling along the track towards some distant hills. wondering what was behind them. Dad jerked me and we walked towards the footbridge, which we crossed to descend onto the other platform.

After a short distance we found a funny little train, just one carriage and a small steam engine. This I learnt much later was the Camden Tram. We joined this diminuitive train, the whistle was blown and the tram was off. Shortly after leaving the yard, the branch line curved to the right, crossed the road and started climbing.

Soon the train was climbing the infamous Kenny Hill, reputedly the steepest adhesion railway in Australia (with grades of 1 in 20 and a short climb of 1 in 19 on the return). The line ran on the northern side of a two lane road and the tram, called *Pansy* by the locals, finally crested the grade and rolled down the other side, puffing along towards Camden— occassionally stopping for people to alight or board the carriage.

At Narellan there was a wig wag warning signal road crossing—one of only two in New South Wales. There was also a huge timber coal loading stage used to load Burragorang Coal into railway wagons.

Seen from afar the little tram could be viewed tripping through green fields, approaching the Nepean River—and finally climbing a slight grade past a milk depot and into the platform at Camden. My uncle's business was just across the road ... you could see it from the plaform.

Later in life Dad collected materials from scrap and built a train set, which we set up in the back room. From humble beginnings it grew and as a young man I and other enthusiasts built 'garden railways'.

I got a job as an apprentice signal electrician on the railways—I journeyed to destinations throughout the system and began taking photographs. As an employee benefit, we were granted free second class passes during the year for holiday travel—and that gave me the means to travel interstate. Mind you, if I learnt how to type, my second class pass would have been upgraded to first!

Many of the photographs in this book are from these trips and journeys.

Throughout my life, I have seen much of Australia via rail and have recorded precious moments where I could. It has also been an interest that has seen me travel internationally— including the US, New Zealand, the UK, France, Switzerland, Italy, Canada and other places.

I hope you enjoy your journey in *Trains and Railways of Australia.*

TRAINS AND
RAILWAYS
OF AUSTRALIA

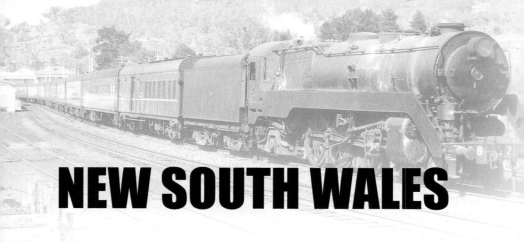

NEW SOUTH WALES

Today the standard gauge for railway tracks in Australia is 1435mm wide, but back in the 1800s a series of recommendations and Acts set the gauge at different widths in NSW and Victoria. How wide to place the rails apart seems to have been an international issue. In England, the *Railway Gauge Act* of 1846 prohibited the construction of future passenger railways other than to the standard gauge of four foot eight and a half inches.

In New South Wales, Mr William Gladstone, Under-Secretary for War and the Colonies, recommended to the legislative council that in the event of railways being constructed in Australia, England's lead be followed and a uniform gauge of four foot eight and a half inches adopted. On 19 February 1850, an Act was passed in South Australia authorising the construction of the Adelaide to Port Adelaide Railway to the four foot eight and a half inch (1435mm) gauge.

However, a newly appointed engineer for the Sydney Railway Company, Irishman Francis Shields, a former city surveyor, urged that the wider five foot three inch gauge, used in Ireland, be adopted for New South Wales. The British Government agreed to the change and a Bill was passed in Sydney on 27 July 1852, stating that the gauge of railways in New South Wales should be five foot three inches. Then on 20 January 1853, Victoria specified the five foot three railway gauge in the *Melbourne and Hobson's Bay Railway Act*. So initially it was all agreed—five foot three would be the standard gauge in Australia.

But as fate would have it Shields resigned over a pay dispute. The new engineer, Scotsman William Wallis, brought with him the latest information from England and Europe, which preferred a four foot eight and a half inch (1435mm) width. As a result, one of his first decisions was to have the 1852 Act repealed and the four foot eight and a half gauge touted as the standard.

By the time this happened, Victoria and South Australia were committed to five foot three, and the dream of a single gauge system nationally would remain just that for many years to come.

The Original Line

On 3 July 1850 the first sod was turned for the railway between Sydney (Redfern) and Parramatta (Granville). The event was a gala occasion with around 10,000 people attending, including some of the finest dignitaries in the colony, including His Excellency Sir Charles Fitzroy. The site, near Devonshire Street, is now known as Sydney Yard.

However, construction was slow, with labour expensive and in short supply because of the migration of people to the goldfields near Bathurst.

Wallis found the explosion of labour costs and other factors that pushed costs out by more than 30 per cent too much to bear and as a result was released from his contract.

Finally, another engineer from England, James Wallace, took charge of the project and made some significant changes. He was unhappy with the timber viaducts on the line and insisted that they be rebuilt with stone and brick. He also made sure that the Sydney to Parramatta project was in part double line railway—and replaced Wallis' timber rails with iron ones.

In January 1854 it was decided that extra money should be found for a branch line to Darling Harbour to coincide with the pending opening of the Sydney (Redfern) to Parramatta (Granville) line.

Go by train
SAFER – CHEAPER

NEW SOUTH WALES RAILWAYS
All Ways and Always the Best Service

Amidst financial chaos, the Government eventually took over the construction of the line in 1855 and by 26 September of that year, traffic began to move along the line after official testing was carried out.

This original Parramatta terminus was near the intersection of Parramatta and Woodville Roads. It wasn't until 4 July 1860 that the line reached the present Parramatta Railway Station, with a deviation to present day Granville. The original Parramatta terminus line would be part of an extension to Liverpool and on to the main Southern Line.

This original line ran a distance of some 14 miles (22 kilometres) with stations at Sydney, Newtown, Ashfield, Burwood, Homebush and Parramatta. It boasted engineering feats including a viaduct over Long Cove Creek (Lewisham), 27 bridges, 50 culverts as well as workshops and station facilities.

The original four locomotives were built by the renowned Robert Stephenson and Co. Works in England.
A composite of them can be viewed in Sydney's Powerhouse Museum today.

Coals to Newcastle

In 1855, the Government took over some private lines being constructed from Newcastle by the Hunter River Company. They were also struggling after beginning construction of a line in 1853.

The coal industry in the Hunter saw a unique mix of early Government and private railways working side by side. Places like Branxton, Rothbury, Richmond Vale and Wallsend all boasted private lines to serve the collieries. Rail heritage is integral to these communities and a number of museums still operate along some of these lines today.

John Whitton's Dream

It was during the early years that one of the most outstanding figures in New South Wales Railways history arrived. John Whitton was appointed engineer-in-chief in January 1857. Whitton had big plans. He wanted to construct railways of the highest engineering quality and expand the system.

While some were touting the idea of horsedrawn railways Whitton successfully argued that this would be a step backward and developed his system of steam traction lines.

Whitton advocated the extension of the existing standard steam lines. Parliament backed him and before long NSW had steam services to Goulburn, Bathurst and Murrurundi. The line to Bathurst would be known as the Great Western Railway (GWR), while Murrurundi would become part of the Great Northern Railway (GNR).

Whitton's dream was to see average speeds on his lines of 40 miles (64 kilometres) per hour—very much faster than road transport.

Across the Great Dividing Range

'Zig Zag' railways were built to cross the Great Dividing Range west of Sydney; one at Lapstone and another between Clarence and Lithgow, which opened in October 1869. It is this second one that was deemed an international engineering wonder for its time, consisting of three major stone viaducts and two tunnels. Today tourists can experience this engineering feat on a narrow gauge line built between the top and bottom of the Zig Zag, built and maintained by the Zig Zag Railway Co-Op.

BELOW The Zig Zag Railway between Clarence and Lithgow, not long after completion in 1869.

The Web Extends

By 1886 railways in New South Wales reached Bourke (the then Main West Line), Narrabri, Glen Innes, Albury, Hay, with branch lines to Jerilderie, Young, Bungandore and Mudgee. The section to Bourke was the longest straight stretch of railway in the world when built, eventually eclipsed by the Commonwealth Railways line across the Nullarbor.

The Hawkesbury was a major impediment to completing a link between Sydney and Newcastle, but by 1 May 1889 the Hawkesbury River was crossed and a direct service between Sydney and Newcastle was finally possible.

The 1920s saw the establishment of a number of 'Pioneer' lines, cheaply constructed branch lines to Kurrajong, Oberon, Batlow, Ballina, Brewarrana, Pokataroo and Coolah. Today community groups at Oberon and Glenreagh are working to keep their local rail heritage alive.

Passengers needing to cross the Clarence River at Grafton would have to wait until 1932 before a bridge replaced the train ferry.

From the original 14 miles in 1855, NSW Railways would traverse 6113 route miles (9387 kilometres) by 1952 with over 5000 of these miles being single track.

Bradfield's Vision for Sydney

The world was looking for efficient alternatives to steam and cities became viable regions to establish and develop electric railways. Engineer Dr John Bradfield had the vision and ability to see Sydney's railways into the future. He oversaw the construction and planning of the Sydney Harbour Bridge, and worked on plans to build a city railway and to electrify existing suburban railways.

Bradfield planned rail extensions to accommodate the city's growth. On 1 March 1926, the first electric passenger train operated between Oatley and Sydney. In the same year, the first part of the Sydney Underground opened with electric trains running to St James. Suburban electrification projects saw services extended to Bankstown and the Royal National Park south of Sydney during that year.

ABOVE The first train to cross the Sydney Harbour Bridge, in 1932. John Bradfield is pictured standing in the front door.

The War and Beyond

During World War II the railways and all who worked on them were overloaded and overworked carrying not only heavy freight and raw materials, but also passengers and military personnel on services known as 'troop trains'. Meanwhile railway workshops concentrated on making war equipment, even weapons such as tanks, aircraft and munitions.

The excessive traffic caused a backlog in maintenance, especially of the tracks, in all states. With the return of men from overseas and a scheme to employ displaced persons from war-torn Europe the maintenance problems were gradually eased.

*The 1950s were truly a golden era in train travel. With the return of peace and the free movement of an increased number of people around the state came the opportunity to build more comfortable trains and
new rollingstock. Main line passenger services were greatly improved
with the introduction of air-conditioned steam trains and two car diesel motor trains for many branch lines. The air-conditioned trains, which in time operated to all major regional centres, included buffet dining cars.
The first of the main line diesel locomotives to haul passenger services were introduced in the mid 1950s. These early locomotives were known as the 40 class and later the 42 class.*

The operation of steam locomotives began to decline in the 1960s, while line electrification reached Bowenfels (beyond Lithgow). By 1962 it was possible to travel between Sydney and Melbourne on one standard gauge train.

From 1974 onwards, with massive fuel shortages, the decline of railway branch lines began and less profitable services were suspended indefinitely. The nature of freight operations changed too. With the regionalisation of depots, the railways ceased being common carriers, while the through freight traffic saw drastic increases in loads. Fast container trains became more popular on interstate routes.

In the new millennium the state government is addressing the need to service the rapid expansion of Sydney with better public transport. Open is a new line between Chatswood and Epping, and planned are extensions into the growing suburbs.

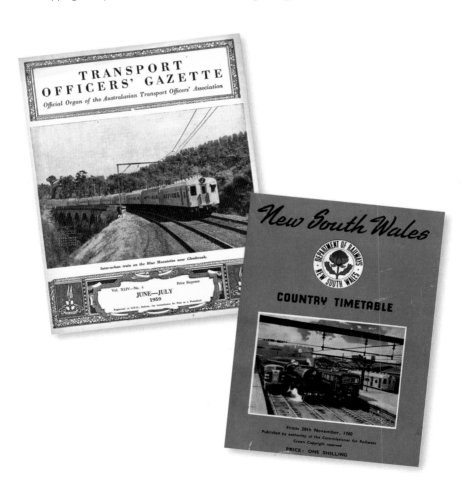

Memories

I have spent much of my life enjoying engineering railway feats in New South Wales. On my first annual leave as a railway apprentice I made much use of my Holiday Pass and travelled extensively around the state.

Waiting to depart in a CPH rail motor to Hay, I was sitting in the seat beside the drivers' cabin. The driver, guard and stationmaster were chatting on the platform. The engine was idling and I glanced into the driver's cab. I noticed a rough stick jamming the foot-operated safety pedal down. The brakes were the only thing stopping the train from moving. At first I thought this was a bit dangerous. But, when the train was running, if the guard was in his centre compartment and the motor ran through one of the tiny platforms en route, he would know something was wrong with the driver and could run through to the drivers' cab and apply the brakes. If an official was coming through from Junee the word would come down the telephone line and the stick would be removed and hidden! The use of the jamming stick saved the driver from leg cramp on the long monotonous journey across the plain to Hay.

Another journey from Narrandera was through Hillston by rail motor to Roto, to connect with the Silver City Comet heading to Broken Hill. I had been warned by a signal electrician who had worked on the line to The Hill that the first thing I would see on the straight track was not the train but a huge cloud of orange dust. True enough—the train appeared from the dust and stopped at the tiny platform and I joined the Comet to continue my journey to the Hill. On the way we stopped in the desert and I stepped out with the breakdown crew to take a photograph. The oppressive heat was like being in a roasting oven. Inside the air-conditioned carriage we were all perspiring and I felt sorry for the crew who were there to repair the draw gear on a disabled Comet carriage on a siding.

Once, I was fortunate to be on the platform at Penrith Station waiting for a train to take me home to Parramatta. Suddenly I heard the sound of a steam loco whistle far different and more attractive than any other I had heard. Shortly there appeared from around the curve, heading towards the station, a large engine painted grey with a conical nose and a headlight in the centre. As it came slowly through the platform, I noted the cab bulging with young workmen in overalls wearing their caps—which they made each morning out of the local newspaper!

Also jammed inside were the officials identified by their suits and felt hats. I later learnt that this engine was 3801, one of five streamlined locomotives built by the Clyde Engineering Company Ltd, at Granville.

Engine 3813 leaving Menangle Park, with the number 50, the early morning train, from Moss Vale. She was one of 25 non-streamlined locomotives of the 38 class and was exhibited at Sydney Terminal, with driving wheels slowly turning, for the NSWGR Centenary celebrations in 1955. Engine 3813 was built at Cardiff, while even numbers in the class were built at Eveleigh. Clyde Engineering built all five streamlined locomotives in the class.
PHOTO: Dale Budd

ABOVE Australia's most travelled and famous locomotive—3801, which first took to the track for trials in January 1943. Fast and powerful, with streamlined looks, she attained the Newcastle to Sydney time record of two hours, one and a half minutes on 28 June 1964 and has travelled as far as Perth, Melbourne and Brisbane.

ABOVE Pacing engine 3528 was originally designed as a passenger express locomotive. This was one of 35 locomotives in the class built at Eveleigh Railway Workshops designed to reduce the need for double heading on mainline express trains.
PHOTO: DENNIS O'BRIEN

BELOW Engine 3823 at Dubbo on the *Coonamble Mail* waiting to depart for Sydney, March 1967. Note the CPH Rail Motor from Gwabegar in the dock platform.
PHOTO: DENNIS O'BRIEN

Engine 3616 with engine 3523 approaching Carabubula hauling a Mixed Goods train on a Saturday in May 1966. Note the Giesl Oblong Ejector (designed to release the exhaust faster) fitted experimentally to where the chimney would normally be. This was the only one fitted in Australia.

PHOTO: DENNIS O'BRIEN

RIGHT For the last time steam hauls the Orange Day Train out of Sydney. The next run will be hauled by a 46 class electric locomotive as far as Lithgow. The engine in this photograph is a 36 class locomotive.

ABOVE A double header; 50 and 38 class locomotives hauling the *Central West Express* up the grade near Springwood in the Blue Mountains. The assisting standard goods engine was attached at Valley Heights, where there was a part roundhouse, turntable and coal and water facilities. With electrification and diesel-electric locomotives, this depot was no longer required. It is now the head office of the NSWRTM
(Blue Mountains Division), which maintains and develops the site and keeps it open for the public.

BELOW These two photographs graphically illustrate why diesel locomotives took over from steam. Taken near the same location, two steam locomotives are needed to haul the heavy air-conditioned train up the steep mountain grades near Springwood, while shortly after, a single diesel loco performs the same task. The loco is 4203, and with it came a new era of rail travel.

The *Southern
Highlands Express*
leaving Sydney Yard
in 1954.
PHOTO: IVAN IVE

38 14

A 36 class locomotive on goods crossing the Macquarie River Bridge, on the Dubbo–Molong line in March 1967.

PHOTO: DENNIS O'BRIEN

Engine 3638 departing Dubbo beneath signal gantry with sheep and general goods in March 1967.

PHOTO: DENNIS O'BRIEN

ABOVE Engine 3668 under the able control of the chief mechanical engineer (steam), the late C A Cardew, on the *Central West Express.* The photo is at the top of the Murrobo Curve just out of Blayney.

BELOW The last *Federal City Express* steam train.

ABOVE Double 36s on western goods. Engine 3655 is assisting—the pilot engine—while the loco behind is known as the train engine.
PHOTO: DENNIS O'BRIEN

RIGHT A 36 class 4-6-0 pilots a 32 class on a goods train on the Main West Line.
PHOTO: DENNIS O'BRIEN

ABOVE Engine 3822 *Central West Express* leaving Sodwalls on 28 August 1965.

PHOTO: DENNIS O'BRIEN

RIGHT Engine 3803 on the number 36 express passenger train, rounding curve at Narara on 24 February 1967. Even-numbered trains were travelling to Sydney and odd numbers were given to trains travelling away from Sydney.

PHOTO: DENNIS O'BRIEN

BLAYNE

CHANCE HERE FOR COWRA
EUCOWRA CRENFELL & HARDE

ABOVE Engine 0-6-0 (referring to the wheel configurations of the locomotive) 1942 shunts at the Darling Harbour Goods Yard on 6 May 1967.

PHOTO: DENNIS O'BRIEN

LEFT Class leader 2701 shunts Rozelle Yard shortly after an overhaul at Eveleigh in 1956.

PHOTO: DENNIS O'BRIEN

ABOVE Tank engine 3093
with a surbuban train on
the long closed Fassifern–
Toronto Branch near
Newcastle.

PHOTO: DENNIS O'BRIEN

RIGHT Empty sheep train
at Gilgandra Railway Station,
March 1967. The engine is
3144; a 30T class locomotive.

PHOTO: DENNIS O'BRIEN

ABOVE Cowra–Blayney goods train leaving Carcoar Tunnel and approaching the railway station behind a standard goods engine.

BELOW Engine 5395 on goods passing Lidsdale State Forest in August 1966.
PHOTO: DENNIS O'BRIEN

ABOVE Engine 5490 and Beyer-Garratt engine 6029 on heavy coal train approaching Tick Hole Tunnel on the refuge road, Cardiff, in July 1963.

PHOTO: DENNIS O'BRIEN

BELOW A glimpse of some of the private lines that operated around NSW, typically to service mining operations and convey passengers.

An SMR 10 class locomotive near Abermain.
These locos were still in service in the 1980s.

PHOTO: UNKNOWN

A shay locomotive on the Wolgan Valley Shale Railway.

PHOTO: A COCKERTON

The Silverton Tramway.

Engine 3801 departing Sydney Yard, before rationalisation.

ABOVE View from the cab of engine 3615 on the *Central West Express,* approaching the Wombool Road Viaduct and heading west in September 1960.

PHOTO: DENNIS O'BRIEN

ABOVE A 57 class engine in the refuge at Springwood cooling its brake shoes during the descent of the Blue Mountins towards Enfield Yard (Sydney).

BELOW Locomotive 5709 running in reverse hauling an empty goods and stock train from Flemington stock yards onto the goods line headed for Enfield Yard.

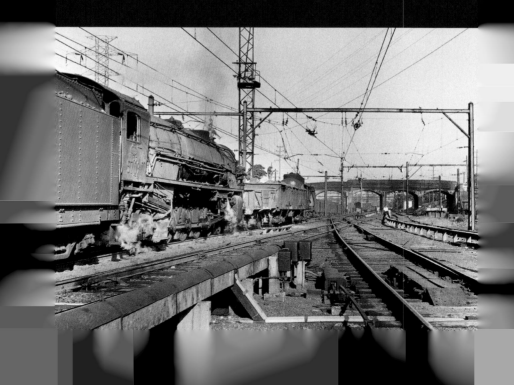

ABOVE Pacing engine 3808 hauling an air-conditioned train.
PHOTO: DENNIS O'BRIEN

BELOW A 35 class locomotive with an 'All stations to Newcastle' train.

ABOVE A 36 class locomotive with a westbound (down) goods through the mainline on Tumulla Bank with another 36 class locomotive assisting in the rear. A 'bank' is a grade on the railway and the rear engine is sometime called the 'bank engine'.

BELOW Also at Tumulla Bank, a standard goods 2-8-0 (wheel configuration) banked by a 36 class 4-6-0.

ABOVE Engine 3811 on the westbound (down) *Central West Express*, leaving the fog as it begins climbing the Blue Mountains.

BELOW Locomotive 3237 passing Clyde Signal Box at speed with a commuter train from Richmond.

RIGHT The *Southern Highlands Express* at Picton where five minutes was allowed for the engine to take water and coal to be shovelled forward to make it easier for the fireman on the long rising grade ahead. Having a clear road the driver is leaning out the cab window for the guard's right-of-way.

BELOW Engine 3646 on the Sydney-bound (up) train, *The Fish*. This was the famous morning commuter train from Mount Victoria. Note the men working on the quadriplication of the line for the coming electrification.

BELOW Engine 3646, this time with its original round top fire box with a short passenger train leaving Sydney Yard.
PHOTO: UNKNOWN

36 46

The *Southern Highlands Express* climbing Spaniard's Hill, early summer.

ABOVE The former Mortuary Station at Rookwood Cemetery. Funeral trains operated from a similar building at Sydney Yard. This building was dismantled stone by stone and moved to Canberra and re-erected as an Anglican church in Ainsley, Canberra. After the re-erection a bell from a Shay locomotive, which operated on the Wolgan Valley Shale Railway near Lithgow, was fitted to the bell tower.

RIGHT Standard goods on worker's train entering Sydney Yard below a now long gone signal gantry. Note compressed air operated route indicators, banner signals and both upper and lower quadrant signals.

ABOVE The era of the steam-hauled commuter trains on the Illawarra Line was drawing to a close when this photograph of superheated 3266 was taken near Waterfall in mid 1964.

BELOW In the winter of 1964 engine 3225 is seen on a Sydney-bound (up) passenger train exiting a tunnel.

ABOVE On the Illawarra Line, engine 3225 exiting a tunnel. This series of photographs was taken not long before the 48 class diesel electric locomotives took over all passenger train working.

...ain...

ABOVE On the edge of the Royal National Park, the detonators have exploded to warn the fettlers to clear the track for the slowly approaching train. The fireman leans from the cab to ensure that no one is standing foul of the up road (track going towards Sydney). Note the smoke drifting slowly upward from the fettler's fire, which is keeping the water boiling for their crib break (morning tea). This photograph was taken in winter 1964 and the engine in the photograph is 3237.

RIGHT A sillouhette of the double Garratt locomotives on the W.44 near Orange.

ABOVE The famous W.44 concentrate train that ran from Broken Hill to Sulphide Junction. On Saturdays it was a very popular train for enthusiasts to photograph, including a number from Melbourne who would share the driving overnight to catch the train somewhere between Manildra and Molong. To Molong the train was normally hauled by a 60 class Garratt piloted by a 36 class locomotive. From Molong to Orange East Fork Junction (as seen here) was W.44 with double Garratts as the motive power—the star attraction.

ABOVE The Garratts passing through the former platform at Amaroo, long since demolished.

LEFT Engine 3675 on W.44 awaiting replacement by the Garratt seen up the yard at Molong with another 36 on a goods train waiting to depart.

ABOVE On the famous Cambelltown to Camden branch line, tank engine 3043 is seen with the usual one carriage as it climbs the infamous Kenny Hill, beside the main road, on grades in excess of one in twenty. The line was believed to contain the steepest unassisted grade in the world.

BELOW Campbelltown back platform was the starting point of the Camden Branch.
PHOTO: RTBU NSW

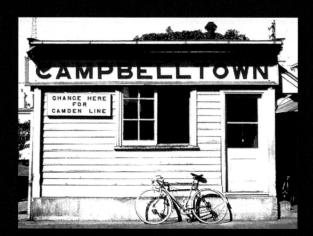

ABOVE Engine 3071 making smoke on Kenny Hill.

PHOTO: IVAN IVE

BELOW The Camden tram.

ABOVE Locomotive 3118 crossing the Nepean River beside the highway nearing Camden.

BELOW A Sydney-bound (up) train climbing near the steep summit of Kenny Hill from where it will virtually roll all the way down to Campbelltown Yard.

A struggling 2029 tank engine on Kenny Hill with a long goods for Camden. It was a wet day and the fireman is belting the sandpipe in an attempt to obtain a flow of sand. onto the rail head. Sand was put on the rails to stop slippage and give the engine traction on the steep grades.

ABOVE Two 30 class locomotives on a Camden bound mixed train approaching Kenny Hill.

ABOVE The return journey the next morning and the engine on the Glenreagh-bound (up) train is seen standing at the fettler's length post. Unfortunately the location was not recorded.

TOP The final ceremonial steam train to Camden climbing Kenny Hill on 1 January 1963 with three 20 class engines including number 2016.

MIDDLE Climbing the scenic Dorrigo branch line out of Glenreagh, there had been heavy summer storms with rain and hail. The only time Engine 1913 (built in 1878) didn't slip on the wet tracks was when it was pasing through the numerous tunnels. In this photograph the train had stalled and as can be seen it had just raised a full head of steam. This train had passenger accommodation in the guard's van. Finally at the last bridge before Dorrigo the engine ran out of steam yet again. The only other passenger, a railway linesman, left the van here and began to walk to Dorrigo station and town.

BOTTOM A standard goods engine with train in tow crosses the Bilesdown Creek Bridge on the Glenreagh-bound (up) journey.

ABOVE An excursion train crossing the bridge after leaving Dorrigo. Note the warning triangle on the post behind the train.

RIGHT Waiting at Phillip stop near the Hawkesbury River on the Kurrajong line. The girls (Jan and Judith) will be waiting some time, with services suspended a few months before in 1952. The sign is now displayed at the Illawarra Light Railway Museum, Albion Park.

ABOVE The same excursion train crossing Bilesdown Creek on the journey to Glenreagh.

ABOVE The Yass Tram, photographed here at the Yass Town platform is engine 1313 with its single carriage. The driver on the right had been noted shovelling coal onto the cab floor. When asked why he said, 'That will last me all day'. Note the conductor's shoulder bag, similar to those used by Sydney Tram Conductors—used for collecting money and selling paper tickets along the route.

ABOVE Seen here in Dutton Street is the Yass Tram with a mixed train between Yass Town and Yass Junction on the Main Southern Line. This train was classified as a tram so that it could be operated by only one man in the cab.

RIGHT Snapped from a passing rail motor returning from Tocumwal—one wonders if anybody ever did! UARDRY was another oddly named stop on the Hay branch. It was the name of a prosperous sheep station.

ABOVE Engine 3016T on a regular mixed train on the Eugowra–Cowra Branch; a return trip connecting with the *Cowra Mail*.

BELOW CPH rail motor in Parkes.

ABOVE Engine 3001, a 30T class locomotive, seen here on the 'Pioneer' Coolah branch line on a mixed train that had connected with the *Mudgee Mail* at Craboon. The line has been long out of use and the engine is in the Rail Transport Museum at Thirlmere. The 'T' on 30T stood for 'tender'—as opposed to a 30 class tank engine.

TOP Sydney-bound *Cessnock Express* moving fast along Mullet Creek trailing a cloud of steam.

MIDDLE The refreshment room, Coffs Harbour. Before the arrival of buffet dining cars, dining cars and XPT buffets in NSW, these Railway Refreshment Rooms were situated strategically to provide meals for passengers on long distance mail trains, expresses and day trains. In NSW a few had hotels upstairs to accomodate rail travellers with inconvenient connections, or cancelled or severely delayed trains. Small refreshment rooms on less frequented lines were leased to private operators.

PHOTO: ROGER MORRIS COLLECTION

BOTTOM Locomotive 3811 with air-conditioned carriages forming the *Northern Tablelands Express* to Mullet Creek.

ABOVE Locomotive 3821 on the Brisbane Limited Express Sydney bound at speed.

BELOW Sydney Station Concourse (the Assembly Platform). The famous destination board on the right is now displayed at the Powerhouse Museum in Sydney.

ABOVE Engine 3612 with the Kempsey Day Train next to Mullet Creek.

BELOW The pride of the fleet. Engine 3801 with the Sydney-bound *Cessnock Express* at Mullet Creek.

ABOVE LEFT Engine 3813 at Eveleigh Locomotive Running Shed. Long demolished, this was the last of three almost identical arched rooved sheds that stood side by side. The sheds were completed in 1885 and could originally accommodate 21 through tracks and house 126 locomotives.

ABOVE RIGHT Engine 3830 and 3813 behind, both in green livery, outside Eveleigh Locomotive Running Shed.

The fettlers working Main Line next to Flemington Car Sidings Signal Box. No safety vests or mechanisation in the late 1950s. Lines were also kept open in those days.

ABOVE A 38 class engine and an 0-6-0 (wheel configuration) engine 1940, a Darling Harbour shunter, outside Eveleigh Locomotive Running Shed.

BELOW Locomotive 3830 on the air-conditioned westbound *Central West Express* passing through Blacktown from the old signal box.

ABOVE At Sydney Station, passenger engine 3823, as well as a 32 and a 36 class locomotive all awaiting their departure signals.

BELOW Billy's last ride. A typically decorated 38 class locomotive (3813) waiting to depart Sydney on the evening *Newcastle Flyer*.

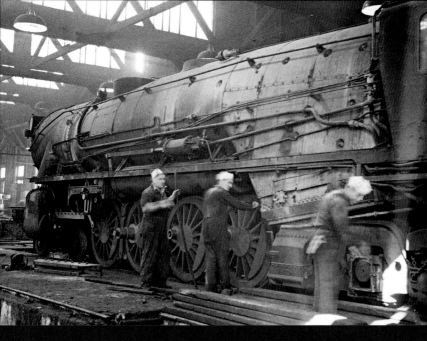

ABOVE Engine 5712 being given a tune-up at the Enfield Workshops..

BELOW A 30 class tank engine (some later given a tender to become a 30T class locomotive) on the Richmond school train on South Creek Viaduct. Note the two 'dog box' carriages coupled behind the engine.

LEFT Diesel engine 7920 imported by the US military service passing Sydney East Box and the carriage sheds known to the yard workers as Bondi Sheds.

RIGHT A 38 class locomotive on the *Central West Express* Sydney bound (on the home stretch) at maximum speed, Seven Hills level crossing.

ABOVE A 400 class rail motor and trailer on a refreshment stop at Jerilderie.

BELOW A near catastrophe! The pay bus had broken down in Glenbrook Gorge, leaving lots of railway workers anxious. This photo shows the most important train in the west being towed into Valley Heights by a steam engine.

ABOVE A mixed train ex Demondrille Junction with Engine 5391 at the front.

BELOW The same train arriving at Young. People on the platform are greeting others or are waiting to join the carriage for Cowra, mid 1964.

ABOVE Engine 3829 in Newcastle being coupled to the air-conditioned *Newcastle Express* cars. The white disc indicates that the engine had been running in reverse from Broadmeadow Locomotive Depot.

BELOW Engine 3203 carrying a coat of arms on an excursion train at Bombo.

A 32 class locomotive hauling a Sydney bound train across the famous Stanwell Park Viaduct, the highest brick arched viaduct in Australia. This scene has been totally destroyed by the electrification of the line and the strengthening with concrete of some of the archways that were in need of reinforcement.

Another photograph of the 3203 excursion train at Bombo showing the station and the proximity to the beach.

ABOVE Aerial view of train number 50, the Moss Vale train behind 3813, not far out of Picton

BELOW The Moss Vale train—number 50 early morning train from Moss Vale—the last regularly hauled steam train in and out of Sydney climbing towards the summit of Menangle Bank. The trail of condensed steam hanging in the cool air, seen through a light mist, traces the route of the railway.

Engine 3136 on the Unanderra Moss Vale train waiting for a clear road to enter Moss Vale.

RIGHT The last of the 4-8-2 steam locomotives—5711—seen leaving Junee for the final time on 23 September 1961. It would soon be the age of diesel and for a few select engines like this one, retirement as a museum piece.

PHOTO: DENNIS O'BRIEN

BELOW Engine 5711 rounding the Bethungra Spiral on its last run from Junee to Goulburn on 23 September 1961. Engine 5711 hauled the first train around the spiral.

Derailment: the pictures tell the story. These shots taken at Wentworthville in early 1964 show 1073, a Craven crane at work.

A 57 class being cut up for scrap.

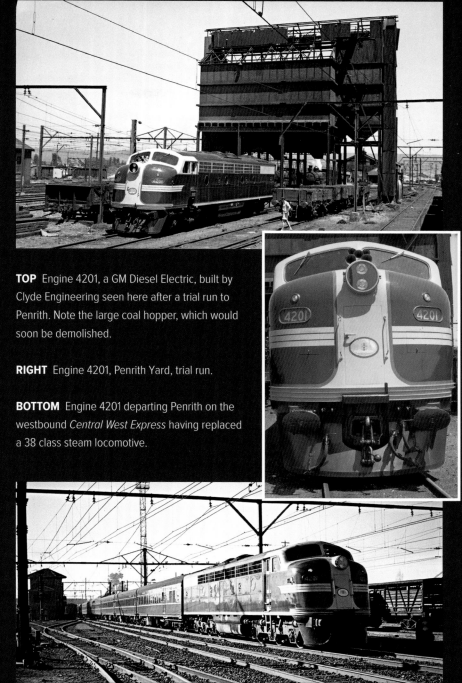

TOP Engine 4201, a GM Diesel Electric, built by Clyde Engineering seen here after a trial run to Penrith. Note the large coal hopper, which would soon be demolished.

RIGHT Engine 4201, Penrith Yard, trial run.

BOTTOM Engine 4201 departing Penrith on the westbound *Central West Express* having replaced a 38 class steam locomotive.

ABOVE Electric locomotive 4612 hauling a set of single deck stainless steel trailer cars. This occurred on passenger runs until sufficient power cars were delivered.

BELOW First electric multiple unit, *The Fish*.

RIGHT The famous *Silver City Comet*, the first air-conditioned train in Australia, powers over Carlacky Creek. A similar train ran between Sydney and Canberra as the *Federal City Express* for some time.
PHOTO: DENNIS O'BRIEN

BELOW The XPT, in NSW.
PHOTO: DENNIS O'BRIEN

Coming soon!
XPT Inter-City Express
Railway into the future

STATE RAIL AUTHORITY OF NEW SOUTH WALES

ABOVE A 30T with a grain train travelling along a country branch line.

OPPOSITE PAGE The Queen and Prince Philip passing through Platform 2 at Parramatta Station on the Royal Train from Bathurst, in 1954.

VICTORIA

As a result of New South Wales passing an Act in July 1852, the gauge of five foot three inches (1600mm) was adopted for the colony. The South Australian and Victorian governments were informed that if they refused to use this gauge they left themselves open to penalties.

So as a result Victoria adopted what would become a five foot three 'broad' gauge. When New South Wales decided to change back to a four foot eight and a half inch (1435mm) system, it was too late for Victoria, as rolling stock and locomotives to fit the broad dimensions had already been ordered.

In 1853, an inquiry was launched in Victoria into which was the most suitable gauge for their state, with the conclusion being that the broad five foot three was indeed the best way for them to go.

The Original Line

The original railway line was constructed from Flinders Street (Melbourne Terminus) and ran to Sandridge (Port Melbourne). The Melbourne and Hobsons Bay Railway Company began construction in January 1853 after being formed the August before. The line was opened on 12 September 1854 and was the first steam locomotive-hauled railway to open in Australia.

Fares to travel on the line were up to a shilling and sixpence, depending which class you rode.

Within three years a line to St Kilda was opened and in a couple more years one to Brighton.

Extensive surveys of Victoria were made for the government's proposed trunk railway system, which with branch lines eventually made up the closest net of railways in Australia. Some key lines included railways between Melbourne and Bendigo, Melbourne and Euchuca and Geelong and Ballarat.

Within a few years Flinders Street, the Melbourne terminus was one of the most ornate station buildings in Australia—an icon for Victorian travellers.

By 1887, it was possible to travel between Melbourne and Adelaide on the *Intercolonial Express*, later named the the *Melbourne Express* when a connection was completed at Serviceton in 1936. This train became known as *The Overland* and still is today.

Victorian Engines

The first locomotive was an improvised ballast engine, followed by an orthodox locomotive built in 1854 by Robertson, Martin, Smith and Company of Melbourne. Over the following decade the system took delivery of a further eleven locomotives, built in England by Robert Stevenson and Company, in Newcastle on Tyne. A further seven locomotives were built by Victorian Railways at Williamstown Workshops in the seven years up until 1879. From 1893 until 1962 an impressive 560 locomotives were built at the Newport Workshops.

The Gauge Goes Through in '62

By 1962 the break of gauge at Albury was eliminated when standard gauge was completed to Melbourne. For the first time a train could run between Sydney and Melbourne without the need to tranship. This was especially welcomed by passengers on the *Southern Aurora*, *Spirit of Progress* and the *Intercapital Daylight*.

The event was heralded by a number of events and functions. A catchphrase reminded passengers of the development: 'The gauge goes through in '62'. This line adorned posters everywhere.

Victorian Curiosities

Victoria also had some unusual narrow gauge lines. The first of them was a two foot six inch (750mm) gauge line between Wangarratta and Whitfield, which opened on 14 March 1899. This line was followed by more narrow gauge operations—between Moe and Walhalla, Colac-Beech Forest and Crowes and Upper Ferntree Gully and Gembrook. This latter line has been lovingly restored and is today one of Victoria's premier tourist attractions, known as *Puffing Billy*.

Victoria also has the distinction of operating the first electric railway system, which (as originally planned) was completed on 15 April 1923, with test runs as early as 1918. The system was later extended into outer suburban areas. In those early years many of the cars that operated the suburban system were steam coaches converted to electric.

Memories

Making use of my interstate holiday pass, I took the train to Bendigo with the intent of riding around the local tram system—most seemed to be hand-me-downs from tramways in Melbourne and Geelong.

On the same pass I journeyed to Ballarat and for the same reason. Ballarat was an interesting station as it had a covered arched roof extending over the platforms and tracks, with an internal footbridge.

Just off the end of the station, I caught a tram that took me onto the main system where I spent the remainder of the day travelling on the numerous routes. I was especially captivated by the single four-wheel tram, which when travelling on the straights did not waver from side to side as it trundled along like the Bendigo four-wheelers did. 'Because we turn the tyres flat,' was the depot manager's explanation.

*It was extremely cold as I waited on the platform at Ballarat for **The Overland** to pull in. I had paid the excess fare to ride by sleeper to Adelaide on this luxury train—the most glamorous in Australia at the time. I walked to the allocated carriage where the conductor greeted me at the door and I showed him my holiday pass.*

He simply said, 'Go down to the next car, mate; the conductor there will fix you up.' I felt a little annoyed by this glib greeting and wondered what kind of carriage I was in for. Nevertheless I was smilingly welcomed and led down the corridor, where the conductor opened the door to a Twinette and said, 'Exclusively yours to Adelaide, sir.' This was sheer luxury—en suite and carpeted floor!

OPPOSITE PAGE *Spirit of Progress* leaving Albury behind one of the streamlined S class locomotives at the end of their long career in 1954. Here it is beginning to build up speed for its non-stop journey to Melbourne.

PHOTO: DENNIS O'BRIEN COLLECTION

ABOVE *Spirit of Progress* departing Spencer Street Platform number 1, circa 1938. *Spirit of Progress* was the prestige train of the Victorian Railways that went into service in 1937. The whole train was built in Australia, at Newport Railway Workshops and all of the steel carriages were air-conditioned. The four S class 3-cylinder engines were built at Newport Workshops between 1928 and 1930 and were streamlined in 1937 to haul this train, which they did until diesel-electrics took over in 1954.

PHOTO: DENNIS O'BRIEN COLLECTION

TOP Interior view of the parlor car attached to *Spirit of Progress*, taken en route between Albury and Melbourne.

BOTTOM *Spirit of Progress* seen at Spencer Street Station in 1954. This train was the first in Australia to carry a hostess to attend to the needs of mothers and children. Here the hostess poses for the camera.

OPPOSITE PAGE

BOTTOM Spirit of Progress at Albury in 1951 with a veteran A2 class locomotive alongside. The A2 class locomotive is waiting to move into the platform after the Spirit departs to form the Albury Express.

ABOVE An overview of Albury Platform showing *Spirit of Progress* ready to depart, with the connecting services from Sydney on the standard gauge track at the right of the photograph.

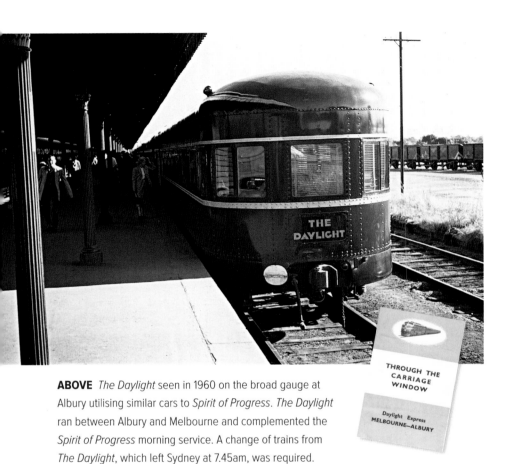

ABOVE *The Daylight* seen in 1960 on the broad gauge at Albury utilising similar cars to *Spirit of Progress*. *The Daylight* ran between Albury and Melbourne and complemented the *Spirit of Progress* morning service. A change of trains from *The Daylight*, which left Sydney at 7.45am, was required.

THROUGH THE
CARRIAGE
WINDOW

Daylight Express
MELBOURNE—ALBURY

LEFT *The Gippslander*, which ran between Melbourne and Bairnsdale. It was electrically hauled to Taralgon—a distance of 97 miles (156 kilometres)— before being diesel-hauled to Bairnsdale.

ABOVE A typical photograph of one of Melbourne's wooden-bodied, swing door electric Tait Trains en route to Essendon. Some of these electric cars were former suburban steam-hauled carriages, known as 'dog boxes'.

RIGHT The blue Harris electric trains were introduced in March 1956 to supplement existing electric stock. Here a Harris train is approaching Flinders Street Station.

ABOVE R class locomotive 725 on the broad gauge passenger train at Albury (The Albury Express) waiting to depart for Melbourne in 1954.

BELOW Another view of the same train at Albury. There were 70 of these locomotives introduced to the Victorian Railways during Operation Phoenix from mid 1951.

ABOVE A D³ locomotive in NSW, arriving from Melbourne at Tocumwal on the day train. Here it will connect with a rail motor for Narrandera.

BELOW At Ballarat Station, built in 1862, a train approaches a signal gantry of lower quandrant type signals.

ABOVE *Mildura Sunlight* arrives at Ballarat Station en route to Melbourne.

LEFT A typical publicity brochure to advertise the recently upgraded *The Overland* —a train that runs between Melbourne and Adelaide. In 2007 Great Southern Railway Ltd converted *The Overland* carriages for daylight use only; They still operate between the two cities.

ABOVE Victoria's famous *Puffing Billy*—with a unique NA class tank locomotive—about to depart Upper Ferntree Gulley for Belgrave. The line had actually closed from Upper Ferntree Gully to Gembrook but a section of the line was reopened thanks to the efforts of the Puffing Billy Preservation Society.

BELOW *Puffing Billy* restored by the Puffing Billy Preservation Society, seen here just after departing from Belgrave. Note the raised 3 foot 6 inch (1067mm) gauge carriages from Mt Lyell Railway in Tasmania that has been converted to 2 foot 6 inches (750mm gauge).

Locomotive NA 7A at Upper Ferntree Gully.

ABOVE A 2 foot 6 inch (750mm) gauge Climax geared locomotive, then out of use, seen here at Erica Sawmill, circa 1954. This locomotive was preserved by the Puffing Billy Preservation Society.

BELOW At Walhalla, a de Cauville saddle tank locomotive after leaving South Melbourne Gas Works. This was an early attempt to restore the Walhalla line, circa 1975. The photo shows the engine shed, built by a volunteer group. The line from Thompson Station has since been restored for tourists and enthusiasts.

The original bridge over the Thompson River.

ABOVE A J class (J 508) goods locomotive in South Western Victoria with a typical goods train of the era heading to Scepton. The J class locomotives were introduced in the mid 1950s.

BELOW An R class coal-fired locomotive double heads with an oil-fired N class locomotive on a goods train bound for Melbourne, circa 1960.

ABOVE Oops! A locomotive 'in the dirt'. An early T class diesel-electric locomotive derailed; seen from the window of the Melbourne-bound express train from Albury.

ABOVE Victorian locomotive B-64 on its delivery run to Albury seen passing through Liverpool Railway Station. Behind the diesel locomotive on the flat car wagon are the broad gauge bogies (pivoted trucks that support the loco) to be exchanged at the border.

ABOVE For Parramatta Civic Week, Clyde Engineering sent a brand new B class locomotive as their contribution. This shot, taken in the former Parramatta Station Goods Yard, illustrates the considerable attention it drew.

LEFT Built between 1905 and 1910, Flinders Street Railway Station is an architectural icon, which inspired other main stations around the world including Luz Station, São Paulo, Brazil. This photograph was taken in the mid 1920s.

THE CLYDE-G.M. DIESEL ELECTRIC LOCOMOTIVE
BUILT FOR THE VICTORIAN RAILWAYS

ABOVE Passing a B class locomotive on a goods train; taken from the Melbourne-bound passenger service from Albury. The loco is B-70 and is on the broad gauge line.

ABOVE Inside the original covered station at Geelong. Note the ornate footbridge, supporting columns and iron work.

BELOW The architectural lines of the new Southern Cross Station in Melbourne, which on completion replaced the old Spencer Street long distance and suburban stations. The station was awarded an Australian Construction Achievement Award in 2007.

ABOVE A Victorian Railways S class locomotive that operated for a time on the privately run West Coast Railway between Melbourne and Warnambool; it did the return trip in a day.

BELOW The waving roof of Melbourne's Southern Cross Station during the early stage of construction.

RIGHT From the Interior of Geelong Station, with the V/Line Train that replaced the West Coast Railway operation.

BELOW A pacing shot of engine R707 returning an excursion train to Melbourne on the North East Main Line. Note the blue Goulburn car behind the locomotive.

ABOVE Engine 3820, which had accompanied engine 3801 on the first steam train between Sydney and Melbourne, with a day excursion train at Spencer Street Station.

BELOW Another shot of 3820 day excursion train.

ABOVE The standard gauge *Spirit of Progress* operating as through train from Sydney with a sleeping car attached, crossing the Maribyrnong River Viaduct.

BELOW Two K class with an excursion train on a branch line returning from Cudgewa on a photo run passing Hume Lake.

ABOVE D³ 639 excursion train.

BELOW Engine K 184 returning from Bright at very slow speed due to the condition of the track.

ABOVE The *Yarra* parlor car crossing a stream on the Bright Line.

BELOW Engine K 184 at the same stream on the Bright Line.

ABOVE Engine D^3 639 on excursion train returning to Melbourne.

Pacing engine R707 returning to Melbourne on an excursion train on the north-east main line.

ABOVE Engine D^3 639 taking water on an enthusiast train.

BELOW Engine D^3 639 on the same tour.

ABOVE Engine K 184 at dusk on the Bright Line tour.

BELOW The Sydney-bound *Southern Aurora* in March 1963. This much-loved train ran between Melbourne and Sydney after the standard gauge opened 16 April 1962. All passengers were accommodated in roomette or twinette sleeping cars and a dining and lounge car was included in each consist. The cars were owned by both the Victorian and NSW railways.
PHOTO: DENNIS O'BRIEN

QUEENSLAND

Queensland's first railway bill was introduced into Parliament on 19 May 1863, only four years after the colony was granted self-government, after a period of debate about which size gauge to adopt. Then Abram Fitzgibbon, an engineer from Ireland, urged the young government to progress with a narrow three foot six inch (1067mm) gauge, arguing that wider gauges would be far more costly to build throughout the mountainous areas and cover the long distances required to service the state's communities. The three foot six gauge system was deemed adequate to meet Parliament's need of an average speed of 20 miles per hour (32 kilometres per hour). The parliament agreed not to follow New South Wales' adoption of a four foot eight and a half inch (1435mm) gauge, instead deciding on their own narrow system.

A Different Design

Early development of the system was to link the cattle farming communities and the many scattered towns along the east coast. However, unlike in other states where the system was designed around the capital city, Queensland built isolated railway sections rather than starting from Brisbane and working out, with many connecting towns and ports, with the view to linking them together as the system grew.

After Fitzgibbon (who would become Queensland's first railway commissioner) won the gauge debate, the first sod was turned on 25 February 1864, for a line between Ipswich and Grandchester (Bigge's Camp). On 25 April 1865, this section was opened shortly after a special preview railway excursion for workers. The first engine to officially run on the line was *Pioneer* and was one of four locomotives bought from the Avondale Engine Company in Bristol, England.

Difficult Terrain

The first real difficulty for the line was when it was extended to cross the Little Liverpool Range, but the line was open by July 1865. Worse was to come with the extension of the line ascending the Great Dividing Range (Main Range) to Toowoomba. This required major

Queensland Railway Refreshment Rooms

Patronise

The Roma Street Cafe
(Including Fruit Stall and Milk Bar)
(OPEN FOR ALL LONG DISTANCE TRAINS)
BREAKFAST, 6/6, LUNCH OR DINNER, 7/6
(Returns Extra)

and **Central Station Cafe**
(Milk Bar and Light Refreshments)
RIGHT ON THE RAILWAY PLATFORMS

QUEENSLAND RAILWAYS
Dining Car Service.
MEAL TICKET.
This Ticket should have Scarlet Corner
attached when placed before Customer
WAITRESS MUST NOT DETACH
SCARLET CORNER.
CHARGE, 6/6

26882

engineering works, including many sharp curves, tunnels and constant steep grades. Descent of this section of the line was no faster than the ascent. Even so, the line opened to Toowoomba on 1 May 1867. Many credit this feat with an influx of several thousand immigrants in 1864 and 1865 from England, with railway construction jobs attracting some of these workers.

The Network Spreads

From Toowoomba, lines radiated across the agriculturally rich Darling Downs to Warwick in 1871, through the higher apple-growing country and eventually to Wallan-garra on the New South Wales border. Also in time there were long reaching lines through Dalby to Cunnamulla and Quilpie.

It was 30 January 1873 when the first sod was turned for a line between Ipswich and Brisbane. In February 1875 the line had opened as far as Oxley Point and in June that year the first train ran from Brisbane to Ipswich. However, it would be July 1876 before the last link between Brisbane and the West—the Indooroopilly Railway Bridge—would open.

At the same time work on a northern rail system had begun and the first section of the Northern Railway between Rockhampton and Westwood was opened on 17 September 1867.

The railway from Townsville to Charters Towers was opened in 1882 and the final linking of the southern and central rail systems occured in 1903.

In the first 50 years, the Queensland Railways had built 4672 miles (7518 kilometres) of line, extending to much of the state. In the next 50 years a further thousand miles of line was built.

The railway from Carins to Brisbane was completed in 1924 with the standard gauge line from South Brisbane to the New South Wales border completed in 1930, allowing trains to travel direct to Sydney.

In the 1930s, Queensland's *Sunshine Express* ran between Brisbane and Cairns—a distance of 1037 miles (1669 kilometres)—three times a week. It wasn't until the late 1950s that the old wooden carriages in service on the run made way for air-conditioned Sunlander trains.

The introduction of diesel-electric locomotives began in 1952 followed by air-conditioned carriages and a complete re-organisation of freight and passenger services.

Queensland Curiosities

The isolated line between Normanton and Croydon, built in 1891, is one of Queensland's railway oddities. This line is now a tourist icon taking people, virtually, from nowhere to nowhere! The 94 mile (151 kilometres) route was originally constructed as a means of carrying gold from Croydon to the Norman River for shipping, but now links these two isolated towns. The line is famous for running on a shoestring budget—the stationmaster is also the driver, engineer and ticket seller!

Not to be forgotten are the 2000 miles (3218 kilometres) of 2 foot (600mm) gauge tramways for the delivery of sugar cane from the plantations to the mills. The many independent systems extended from Nambour in the South to Mossman in the north. The sugar from the Mossman Mills was taken by 2 foot gauge tramway to Port Douglas for export. This line also carried general freight and, for a time, passengers.

Memories

My first journey into Queensland by rail was with an apprentice friend and we travelled on a Holiday Pass. We went via the Great Northern Railway in New South Wales on the **Brisbane Express**. Leaving Sydney at 1.55pm on a Friday, this train, number 17, could hardly be called an express as it stopped at many stations until Armidale. From there it stopped at all stations passing over the highest point of any railway in Australia about 1 mile (1.6 kilometres) south of Ben Lomond Railway Station where the altitude is 4517 feet (1376 metres).

The 'Express' arrived at Wallan-garra at 7.50am and here we had breakfast, which we both agreed was the worst we had ever had in any refreshment room! Of interest was that the Queensland–New South Wales border runs across the platform, leaving doubt as to which state the station belongs to.

The short Queensland Railways train, hauled by a steam engine, probably a B18¼, though we were not conversant with the classes of interstate locomotives. The train spent much of its time descending and we passed through the apple-growing areas near Stanthorpe.

At one point, the train stopped on the side of a rolling hill. After a time I looked out the window and there were the driver, fireman and guard sitting on the far rail of a crossing loop having their crib break. The boiling water in the billy had been obtained from the steam engine. As the train was definitely pointing downhill we were hoping that the crew had securely fixed the brakes!

Once past Warwick the driver urged the engine to gallop the train across the flat and fertile Darling Downs. We had carefully worn goggles to protect our eyes from the soot and embers. We didn't realise how effective this protection was until we lifted the goggles rolling into Toowoomba to reveal white circles on two very blackened faces! For the spectacular descent down the Main Range our engine had been exchanged for an almost new diesel-electric locomotive. We finally reached Brisbane after 6pm. Today you can fly to London in less time, while the XPT rail journey between Sydney and Brisbane has cut the time to around 14 hours.

LEFT Arched station on the isolated Normanton—Croydon Railway.

PHOTO: UNKNOWN

ABOVE Moreton Central Mill: An empty cane train crossing the Bruce Highway. Cane trains no longer run at Nambour. It was, in its day, the most southerly cane tramline system in Queensland. Cane trains or cane trams ran mostly on a narrow 2 foot gauge—of which there were almost 2000 miles (3218 kilometres) in the state.

BELOW This lifting bridge was part of the Moreton Central Mill system and allowed river traffic to pass when there were no cane trams using the line.

ABOVE The Coolum crossing the Bruce Highway in Nambour.

BELOW The out-of-use Shay locomotive, which was later preserved, in Moreton Central Mill Yard.

ABOVE Central Station.

ABOVE At Brisbane Central Station, engine 1035 (Class BB18 1/4) is about to depart with a suburban train to Shorncliffe. The platforms at Central Station have long been covered by a shopping centre.

ABOVE The former Roma Street goods yards and station in the late 1950s. Much of this area has been transformed into a tropical park.

BELOW Engine 778, with additional water supply behind the engine, on a ballast train on the Dungardon Branch, near Ipswich in the late 1950s.

BELOW At Ernest Junction on the South Brisbane to Southport Line, the connecting train is ready to depart for Tweed Heads just across the border. The PB 15 engine will travel through what is now the Gold Coast Hinterland and some formations near Mudgeeraba. This line was closed for many years and then replaced by an electrified line from Beenleigh to Robina. It is now possible to travel by electric train from Robina, through Roma Street Station, to Brisbane Airport.

ABOVE At Ipswich before the station was covered by a commercial precinct and the line was electrified; a steam train on the main platform and a rail motor perhaps connecting for a run further west.

BELOW Descending the main range from Toowoomba, an early Queensland Railways Main Line diesel-electric approaches the famous Spring Bluff crossing loop, always ablaze with flowers, particularly for the Toowoomba Spring Festival. The station is no longer attended; however, the flower gardens are still maintained.

ABOVE A suburban train leaving the original Indooroopilly Bridge for Roma Street in the late 1950s. The new bridge, painted in a red priming coat, has been constructed for quadriplication of the line.

ABOVE The 8.55am rail car set leaving Maryborough for Urangan in the late 1950s.

BELOW Making up a goods train in Maryborough Yard, note the signal cabin and the bypass line to the right of the engine. This allowed through trains to bypass the terminal platform at Maryborough.

ABOVE The Buderim Tramway near Nambour.

PHOTO: UNKNOWN

BELOW The day train to Brisbane waits in the dock platform at Bundaburgh. It stopped at all stations to Caboolture. Fortunately this train has been replaced by the electric trains operating between Brisbane and Rockhampton.

PHOTO: UNKNOWN

Just south of Gladstone, this Sunlander has come to grief after colliding with a trolley load of rails.

ABOVE Rescued by a steam engine that was working in Gladstone Yard, the train continues its journey to the station. Interestingly in Queensland and Western Australia, the driver operates the locomotive on the right-hand side of the cab.

RIGHT A newspaper report, detailing the incident.

D., SEPT. 4, 1957. FIVE

SUNLANDER IN COLLISION

INCIDENT NEAR GLADSTONE

FIREMAN'S NARROW ESCAPE

GLADSTONE, Sept. 3.—A railway fireman narrowly missed death to-day when a 24 foot length of steel rail smashed through the driving cabin of the Sunlander near Gladstone, just missing his head.

The fireman was Stewart Leslie Jarrett of Bundaberg, who was in the cabin of the Sunlander when it was involved in a collision with a flat-top railway trolley loaded with 24 foot steel rails.

The north-bound Sunlander was running 40 minutes late and was about a mile south of Gladstone when the collision occurred about 10.30 a.m. The impact of the collision, which was heard about half a mile away, smashed the flat top and hurled it off the line.

A 24 foot length of steel tore through the front of the Sunlander cabin, just missing Jarrett's head and penetrating the roof of the cabin. Several sleepers were gouged out by lengths of steel, some of which were bent into a U-shape.

Eye-witnesses said the 450-ton Sunlander had slowed down just before the impact and pulled up in little more than its own length and few of the passengers realised that the collision had occurred.

Following the collision, the rail which penetrated the cabin was cut from the engine, leaving a section of 12 feet still embedded in the bodywork. The Sunlander's diesel was towed into the Gladstone yards by a steam engine and was later brought to Rockhampton for repairs. Another diesel was connected to the Sunlander which resumed its journey to Townsville after a delay of about an hour.

ABOVE Beyer-Garratt 1097 resplendent in maroon with yellow lining direct from the Mayne Locomotive Workshops in Brisbane. It is seen here at the Rockhampton Coal Stage and will, like the other Garratts based there, never be cleaned again!

LEFT A Beyer-Garratt engine on an empty stock train taking water heading west to Emerald, the limit of the working for Garratts.

As there were insufficient air-conditioned cars to operate a full Sunlander service, on certain days the *Sunshine Express* still operated. Seen here at St Lawrence, north of Rockhampton, the train is making a meal stop at the refreshment room as there was no dining car on the *Sunshine Express*.

BELOW Interior of one of the carriages.

PHOTO: UNKNOWN

ABOVE The safe working staff is handed to the fireman of a Garratt engine about to leave on a freight train to the Mount Morgan Line.

BELOW Climbing the deviation of the line to Mount Morgan. The original line climbed steep grades using the ABT (rack railway) system, the only such rack system in Australia at the time, other than the Mount Lyell Railway in Tasmania. The deviation replaced the 1 in 16 grade rack railway in 1952.

ABOVE Rockhampton Railway Station in 1961. Note the corrugated iron construction of the original building, which opened in 1867. The station is now completely unrecognisable after being rebuilt as a modern facility and is the terminus of the longest electrified line in Australia.

LEFT The platform side of Rockhampton station with a somewhat elegant roof.

ABOVE At the Archer Park end of Denison Street, Rockhampton is what was known as the Yeppoon Flyer. Note the PB 15 engine, which was fastidiously kept polished by the engine crew between journeys, except if it rained!

BELOW Another view of the Yeppoon Flyer. This morning and afternoon commuter train was noted for passengers alighting or entraining in the street.

ABOVE This is a C17 class locomotive with a goods train in Denison Street slowly approaching Rockhampton Station. Note the fireman leaning out his window loudly ringing a hand bell to warn people of the approaching train. The C17s were known as Brown Bombers.

BELOW Engine 891 departing Rockhampton Station on a goods train. Note the driver taking the hand bell from the signalman as the train departs.

ABOVE In Denison Street, Rockhampton a then modern 2000 class stainless steel rail motor.

LEFT A Rockhampton-bound goods train from Emerald approaching a tunnel.

RIGHT The same train leaving the tunnel.

BELOW The electric Tilt Train at the modern Rockhampton Station. With a service speed of 163 kph (100 mph) the Queensland Railway Tilt Trains are the fastest narrow gauge trains in the world. The electric Tilt *City of Rockhampton* reached 210 kph (130 mph) on a speed test in 1999.

ABOVE A Cairns-bound diesel Tilt Train from Brisbane waiting at Ingham. The diesel Tilt Trains operating between Brisbane and Cairns have the same maximum service speed, are all business class (bettering most airlines) and have TV screens stowed in an arm of each seat. Travellers may watch late release movies and other programmes.Music is also available with all sound through ear-phones. The screens also show the location of the train and distance to next stop. A unique feature is Driver Cam—a camera fitted into the power car cab that shows the track ahead at day and night!

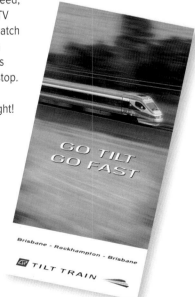

GO TILT
GO FAST

Brisbane - Rockhampton - Brisbane

QR TILT TRAIN

ABOVE A Sunlander arriving at Cairns in mid 1954.
Note the various rail motors to the left of the photograph.

BELOW From the front of a rail car arriving at Redlynch on the Cairns Railway
at the foot of the climb to the Atherton Tableland.

ABOVE A group of workmen and their families, doubtless just after the completion of the Stoney Creek Viaduct (probably the opening) on the Cairns to Kuranda line, 21 miles (34 kilometres) long and constructed in the late 19th century. It took four years to build, has 15 tunnels, the Stoney Creek Viaduct, a number of short timber trestles clinging to the side of the Barron Gorge and 93 curves. Twenty workmen lost their lives while constructing this engineering masterpiece, which was completed in 1888.

PHOTO: UNKNOWN

OPPOSITE PAGE A tourist train on the Stoney Creek Viaduct with some of the passengers walking ahead to a lookout built for people to photograph the special trains with the waterfalls in the background.

PHOTO: UNKNOWN

ABOVE One of the many varieties of Queensland Railways rail motors with a trailer; at Barron Falls Lookout where the tourist train stopped.

ABOVE A steam-hauled special train from Cairns carrying tourists from the liner *Duntroon*, which normally sailed between Sydney and New Zealand. The train is at Barron Falls Station.

BELOW Barron Falls as seen from the railway lookout. Since then, an irrigation dam has been built upstream so that the flow of water is little more than a trickle except during the wet season.

ABOVE The famous Kuranda Station, a tourist legend in Far North Queensland. This line is arguably the most scenic railway in Australia. Noted for its immaculately tended flower gardens and tropical foliage the station is one of the most photographed destinations in the region. The rail motor train is waiting to return to Cairns.

BELOW The *Duntroon Special* steaming on to Kuranda at the head of the gorge and the top of the Barron Falls.

ABOVE A rather different rail motor with a van coupled behind it photograhed on the Cooktown–Laura Branch line. The chassis of this rail motor and the engine were actually from a London bus. The author saw an embossed brass sign on what had been the top of the steering column which read: 'This bus must not be operated within "X" miles of London'. Operating between Cooktown and Laura was surely outside of the permitted zone! The engine drove through a manual gearbox to the larger diameter rear wheels and overall the ride was rather rough! Tourists travelled from Cairns to Cooktown by boat then caught the rail motor to Laura and returned on a day trip.

ABOVE On the return journey from Laura the motor is seen setting back across the dry Deighton River. The author arranged with the driver to back across the trestle then run forward to film with his movie camera. The driver was also the station master at Cooktown and was very keen to see the line kept open as a tourist attraction. He stopped twice on the return to lead us into the bush to point out rare features he had discovered. The line was closed soon after, in 1961.

BELOW Rail motor and trailers at a refreshment stop at Guthalungra en route to Bowen from Townsville.

ABOVE The Emu Park Branch line near Rockhampton—closed, as were many branch lines in the state. Seen here is the abandoned engine shed, water tank, buffer stops and a few of the town's shops. The rails have long been removed by the time this photograph was taken in the mid 1960s.

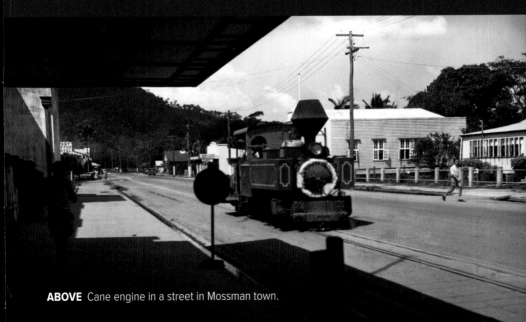

ABOVE Cane engine in a street in Mossman town.

The Balley Hooley Railway at Port Douglas Marina running on the former Mossman to Port Douglas Tramway, which carried bagged sugar from the Mossman Central sugar mill to the Port Douglas Jetty for export. The 2 foot gauge tramway originally ran beside the gravel road between the two settlements. In addition to carrying sugar and other freight, this line also carried passengers. The line opened in August 1900. Today it operates as a tourist service at

WESTERN AUSTRALIA

T he first locomotive in Western Australia was named *Ballaarat* after the Victorian city in which it was built. It first ran in 1871 and served a timber line through an area known as 'Kingdom of the Karri', running between Lochville on the coast (near Busselton) and Yoganup. The engine was supplied and operated without a cabin for the crew, but in true Australian style, one was later tacked on the engine frame using corrugated iron!

The railways in Western Australia are characterised by the three foot six inch (1067mm) gauge government system and the mostly private timber lines that served the many districts. The abundant jarrah trees were used as sleepers for the early railway lines.

Private Lines

Private trunk lines were successful—unlike early private railways in other states—partially because of a land grant system that was devised for the builders along the route of the corridors.

The Great Southern Railway and the Midlands Railway were built and operated by private enterprise. Under the deal, both the Midland and the Great Southern Railway Company were given 12,000 acres of land per mile of railway to the east and west of the corridor in return for building the line. This gave the backers of the Great Southern Railway—a 243 mile (391 kilometre) line—almost 3 million acres of real estate.

MEET THE "Westland"

WESTERN AUSTRALIAN GOVERNMENT RAILWAYS

ABOVE Typical scene of a bush railway in Western Australia. State Saw Mills Locomotive SSM No 8 on the Pemberton Bush Line.

The Great Southern Railway

The dream of a great southern railway was originally promoted by Anthony Hordern, a well-known Sydney retailer, who was keen to open up a route between Albany and Perth. The roads were terrible, and typically a journey would take anywhere between a week and 16 days. Anthony Hordern died before his grand plans to open up the south came to fruition, but the Great Southern Railway did open on 1 June 1889. In 1896 the government took over the line after the private company fell into financial difficulty because of a monetary crisis experienced by their backers in London.

The Midlands Railway

The story was different for the Midland Railway Company. They chose their land well, and they developed railway stations along a route from the capital to the port for the Murchison goldfields. Work began on the Midland Railway in 1886 and work was completed in 1894. The company operated the line until 1964, when the Western Australian Government finally took over operations.

The Network Spreads

The railway finally reached Perth in 1881 by way of a government line. By 1885 it had extended 90 miles (144 kilometres) into the Avon Valley. In the late 1960s the Avon Valley line was converted to dual (narrow/standard) gauge and features some of the deepest cuttings in the country.

By 1896 the railway had reached Kalgoorlie bringing to the far flung mining town water for four pence a gallon.

Western Australian Government Railways also had an isolated line known to locals as the Spinifex Flier. Opened on 1 July 1912, it stretched over 100 miles (160 kilometres), joining Marble Bar and Port Headland.

ABOVE V class locomotive at East Perth Loco.

PHOTO: WAGR

Mining and Expansion

Today, railways in Western Australia have revolutionised mining in remote regions to the north of the state, with standard gauge trains the longest and heaviest in the world carrying ore to ports. This new generation of freight-carrying trains has been part of the story of enormous wealth in Western Australia.

Western Australia today has a progressive public railway expansion programme, with a new extension from Perth to the north and to Mandurah. These suburban electric railways are part of an overall plan to ensure Perth and surrounds has a public transport system able to cater for the needs of the expanding city.

Perth sets an example to all other capitals in mass transit. The Northern Line, with a double track electrified railway in the median of a highway, opened up large areas of land for homes many near beaches.

Recently it has been extended and now has lengthened platforms and enlarged car parks for park and ride. In December 2007 a similar line was opened to Mandurah in the south. This electrified line is known as the Southern Suburbs Railway and cost $1.66 billion, with construction beginning in 2002. The 72 kilometres electrified line has two underground stations in the city served by 774 metres of twin tunnels and nine more including the Mandrah terminus. Bridges and structures were built or modified, including an added rail bridge to the Narrows Bridge and widening of the Mt Henry Bridge. The tracks run along the median of the Kwinana Freeway, through Kwinana and Rockingham and on to Madurah.

On the standard gauge line, Perth to Kalgoorlie, the self-powered diesel train named *The Prospector* runs at a service speed up to 163 kph (100 mph), which is the same speed as the Queensland Railway Tilt Trains, but without the tilting equipment. This equals the fastest train speed in Australia. Some days it is tabled to make the return trip in one day.

Memories

*Returning from Perth on **The Westland** was an experience that has remained etched in my memory. The long train was hauled by an X class diesel-electric locomotive as far as Midland Junction, where it stopped. Unbeknown to me, a steam locomotive was coupled to the X class as an assistant engine ready for the climb up the Darling Range.*

There was a certain amount of hooting and whistling before the train was away again, and before long we reached the foot of the range and began the ascent. When the complete train was on the grade, I felt a violent slip of the steam engine and rushed across the corridor, thrusting my head out the open window.

The engines had made a left-hand curve, so I was almost looking side on at the locomotives from my position in the long train. The diesel-electric was clearly in trouble and not hauling its share of the load, so the steam engine (class unknown) was being worked hard by its crew in a valiant attempt to haul the train up the range, slipping wildly.

A surprising sight was the diesel blowing perfectly shaped smoke rings or doughnuts from its exhaust, although I couldn't hear any exhaust sound because of the herculean effort being made by the assistant engine. Apparently this was a regular occurrence for the X class.

*Soon it was dark, and as we were on a single line, I wondered just how we would be rescued from this predicament. It was important for **The Westland** to reach Kalgoorlie close to its scheduled time because of its connection with the **Trans-Australian Express**.*

*After some time, there was a chorus of exploding detonators, steam engine whistles and diesel sirens, and soon we began to move up the range. In the dark we reached a small station and there on the track on the other side of the V platform was the **Albany Progress**, with its club car lit up illuminating waiting passengers enjoying a soothing drink. **The Westland** had been rescued as quickly as possible to minimise delays to its passengers proceeding on the **Trans-Express**.*

ABOVE Abandoned Northam Station looking west in 1970, after the new Avon Valley Line opened in 1966.

BELOW Northam Station was served by a short branch line to Spring Hill on the Great Southern Railway to serve the flour mill and fuel depot.

ABOVE Spencer Brook platform in 1970, the former junction of the main line to Perth and the Great Southern Railway. It was closed early in 1966. However, iron ore trains to Wundowie continued to run through until 1981.

BELOW Locomotive S545 on the Western Australian Government Railway (WAGR) Reso train in 1970. Photographed from South Western Highway between Boyanup Junction and Dardanup.

ABOVE Engine W931 double heading with S545 on the same train. This highway is now called the Boyanup–Picton Road.

BELOW The Reso train at Boyanup Junction at the Bunbury end of the yard. The train was heading for Bunbury.

ABOVE Engine S545 with Locomotive W931 double heading on the Reso train leaving the north end of Bridgetown yard, heading to Bunbury.

ABOVE At Collie, locos that were stowed mid 1970. They were written off in 1971–1972 and scrapped between 1972 and 1974.

BELOW A W class in steam at Collie yard alongside the coal stage.

ABOVE A view of Hillman Yard workings; crossed goods train leaving the loop.

BELOW North end of Hillman yard looking South. Engine S546 with a goods train is taking water. Note train which has left the loop in the background.

ABOVE Bunbury-bound goods train at North End of Donnybrook yard.

BELOW Engine V1206 leaving Midland Junction with a short goods train.

PHOTO: JOHN JOYCE

A V class locomotive between Swan View and National Park with an eastbound goods to Northam; around 1962.

PHOTO: WAGR

Locomotive V1216 on the old Eastern Railway. The Vs were the largest non-articulated three foot six inch gauge engines in Australia.

PHOTO: WAGR

ABOVE *Australind* hauled by diesel-electric engine X1004 at Pinjarra Station looking south, once the fastest narrow gauge train in Australia.

BELOW Engine PMR 727 at Old Bunbury Station ready to depart for Perth overnight with produce from the Bunbury area.

ABOVE Bunnings locomotive number 86 at Donnelly River Mill 20 kilometres north west of Manjimup.

LEFT State Saw Mill locomotive SSM Number 8 hauling logs; Pemberton Bush about 10 kilometres South East of Pemberton.

ABOVE Engine Cs 439 on Murray River Bridge (Asquith), northbound with logs for Banksiadale Mill.

RIGHT Engine Cs 270 (Black Butte) on the Murray River Bridge heading north with logs for Banksiadale Mill.

ABOVE Engine Cs 439 (*Banksia*) on the Banksiadale bush line.

BELOW Engine N200 at Armadale with a Railway Historical Society Special
PHOTO: WAGR

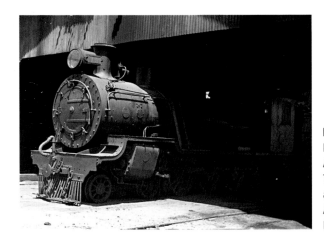

LEFT The Midlands Railway of Western Australia—Engine D19. The Midlands Railway was absorbed by the Western Australian Government Railways in 1964.

BELOW Locomotive CS436 approaching Banksiadale Mill from the north. This locomotive was only briefly at the mill in the early 1950s and was not named.
PHOTO: WAGR

ABOVE WAGR diesel-electric locomotive built at the English Electric Rocklea, Brisbane Plant. For a public relations exercise it hauled goods trains from Brisbane through Sydney to Perth.

PHOTO: ENGLISH ELECTRIC COY

BELOW Engine DD596 between Subiaco and Daglish; bound for Fremantle from Perth.

ABOVE Perth Station in 1962. Note the DD tank engine with steam up about to leave with a suburban train and three diesel-powered suburban trains. This scene is very different today.

The old days. Constructing the main Rio Tinto train line between Tom Price and Dampier in the mid-1960s.

PHOTO: RIO TINTO IRON ORE

ABOVE Rio Tinto iron ore train in the Pilbara.

RIGHT Two Rio Tinto iron ore trains passing on one of the giant Pilbara rail haulage lines, which amount to over 800 miles
(1300 kilometres).

TASMANIA

I have travelled to Tasmania several times to photograph the many unique lines; however, when it comes to the history of the railway systems, I could not go past the expertise of my long time friend Jim Stokes. Jim has kindly provided the following introduction to Tasmania.

Rail services in Tasmania began in 1871 with the opening of the privately owned five foot three inch (1600mm) gauge Launceston–Deloraine line. In 1876 the Tasmanian Main Line Railway completed a three foot six inch (1067mm) gauge line from Hobart to Launceston. This joined the Deloraine line at Western Junction and continued into Launceston, utilising a third rail laid on the Deloraine line. The Tasmanian Government took over the Deloraine line in 1873 and the Main Line in 1890, forming the basis of the Tasmanian Government Railways (TGR). Between 1885 and 1892 the TGR extended its three foot six inch gauge system to Sorell, Glenora, Apsley and Oatlands in the south, St Mary's and Scottsdale in the north-east and Mole Creek and Ulverstone in the north-west. There were further extensive additions to the system in the first quarter of the 20th century. The Glenora line was extended to Fitzgerald, the Scottsdale line to Herrick and the Ulverstone (Western) line to Burnie, Stanley and Smithton. Branches were built off the Western line to Roland, Barrington, Nietta, Maweena, Trowutta and Marrawah.

Mining in the West

The mining districts on the West Coast were served by a mixture of TGR and private lines. In 1878 the Van Diemen's Land Coy built a three foot (915mm) gauge wooden-railed horse tramway from Burnie to Waratah. This was converted to a three foot six inch (1067mm) in 1884 and in 1900 it was extended south to Zeehan as the Emu Bay Railway. Zeehan had already been linked with the port of Strahan by a TGR line in 1892 and the through route from Burnie to Queenstown was completed in 1901 when the Mt Lyell Mining and Railway Coy's Abt rack railway from the copper mines at Queenstown was linked with the TGR at Strahan. The rival North Lyell copper mine built a separate three foot six inch (1067mm) gauge line from Linda to Kelly Basin on Macquarie Harbour. There were also numerous 2 foot (610mm) gauge lines

on the West Coast, notably a combined TGR and private network in the Zeehan area and an extensive system operated by the Mt Lyell Coy in the Queenstown area.

Trains for Difficult Terrain

Railway operation in Tasmania was never easy. The mountainous terrain increased construction costs and reduced operating speeds, while the proximity of much of the population to seaports made it harder for rail to compete with road. However, the system was well served by the locomotives built in its earlier years by Beyer Peacock of Manchester and from the 1920s by the large Q class 4-8-2s and R class 4-6-2s built in Australia. Beyer Peacock also built the world's first two Beyer-Garratt articulated locomotives in 1909 for the TGR's 2 foot gauge Zeehand–Williamsford line. The Emu Bay Railway also used Garratt locomotives extensively. From the 1920s the TGR introduced petrol, steam and diesel railcars to meet growing road competition. Several branch lines were also closed between 1926 and 1931, as was the North Lyell Railway.

Passenger Services

Industrial development in Tasmania from the 1930s brought increased freight traffic and in the 1950s the TGR undertook a major rehabilitation program, including Australia's first fleet of diesel-electric locomotives, new wagons and articulated diesel railcars. The railcars introduced the *Tasman Limited* passenger services between Hobart, Launceston and

Wynyard in 1954. Steam locomotives were gradually eliminated, although some remained in use until the early 1970s. Most of the smaller branch lines were closed between 1947 and 1963 and the Mt Lyell Railway also closed in 1963.

Moving with the Times

The 1970s were a decade of major change. The establishment of the export woodchip industry led to the completion of a new line from Launceston to the port of Bell Bay in 1974 and a big increase in timber traffic over most of the system. In 1978 the Commonwealth Government's Australian National Railways took over the TGR system and set out to cut costs radically by reducing staff, ending the remaining passenger services, concentrating on bulk freight and importing second-hand locomotives and wagons from the mainland. The Commonwealth sold the former TGR system to a private operator in 1997 and the same operator purchased the Emu Bay Railway in 1998. The following decade was the most difficult in the history of the system, with changes of operator, loss of traffic to road, increasingly rundown track and rolling stock and threats to close most of the system. By 2008 the closure threat appeared to have been averted and progress made on funding for rehabilitation. However, the only lines in current operation were the main container route from Hobart and Boyer (Derwent Valley) to Bell Bay and Burnie, the Emu Bay line for the West Coast ore traffic and the Conara Junction–Fingal line for coal traffic.

Memories

I have fond memories of the variety and uniqueness of the different railways in Tasmania and the wonderful hospitality of the locals. On one train, my mate Don and I were invited to ride in the cab on the way to Launceston from Herrick. This was a wonderful example of the crew's hospitality. At one stage we were passing a cemetery and the driver shouted, 'The engine derailed here last week!' Apparently the new engine flanges were pushing the rails apart.

Later we began a stiff climb to a tunnel and witnessed a fine example of mateship. Bruce, the driver, left his seat and took the shovel from his fireman—no words could have been heard over the roar of the climbing engine. Bruce began scooping coal from the tender and expertly hurling it into the firebox, giving his mate a chance to rest. As we approached the tunnel the Irish fireman dipped sweat rags into a bucket of water, squeezed them, then handed them to me and Don, indicating we should hold the cloth as a filter across our nose and mouth.

Almost instantly we plunged into the tight tunnel and quickly realised the reason for the fireman's thoughtfulness—steam and cinders streamed back into the cab. The fireman knew we were being met by two young ladies and he wanted us to look our best. It was dark and the train was late as we approached Launceston Railway Station. He rinsed the sweat rags again, presented a cake of soap and dry cloths, and suggested we should 'scrub up' for the waiting girls!

During the **West Coaster**'s stop at Guildford I was checking out the modern updating of the livery of the near ancient Dubs steam loco of the E.B.R. The driver spotted me. 'Like a ride?' he called and I almost tripped in my rush to climb into the cab. 'Take the seat behind me on the tender. You'll have a smoother ride.' I did so, because I remembered how rough it was riding 36 and 38 class engines at home. They bucked so much I sometimes wondered if they were still on the rails!

We were off. As the Dubs was an oil burner now, the fireman had little to do. Soon we began the descent into the Pieman River Gorge with its continuous sharp curves, many through cuttings. The little engine bucked and swayed and I noticed something a little frightening... The driver was sitting on his seat, leaning his back on the cab wall for stability with his feet up on the brake column; he'd pulled the folded morning paper from his back pocket and was reading! Neither the driver or fireman was watching the twisting track ahead.

I yelled to the driver: 'Isn't this a bit dangerous?'

'Naw. If I drove slow enough to stop short of any obstruction we'd meet ourselves coming back from Zeehan and the passengers would be upset at being late. The boss wouldn't like that.' And with that he turned back to read his paper.

OPPOSITE PAGE An un-rebuilt A class locomotive 4-4-0 at mainline platform, Launceston in the early 1920s. It is the Launceston (King's Wharf) to Hobart boat train.
PHOTO: UNKNOWN

ABOVE An A class locomotive 4-4-0 (wheel configuration) possibly at Westerway, Derwent Valley, 1920s. PHOTO: UNKNOWN

BELOW An R class engine 4-6-2 (wheel configuration) at Launceston, circa 1944. PHOTO: TGR

ABOVE An R class locomotive 4-6-2 (wheel configuration) Pacific on a Launceston to Hobart morning express between St Leonards and Western Junction in 1947.

PHOTO: TGR

BELOW A westbound goods crossing the Ballahoo Creek, just west of Latrobe, circa 1947.

PHOTO: TGR

A special school picnic train at Launceston waiting to depart for Rocherlea on the North–East Line.

BELOW Another view of the special school picnic train.

ABOVE Train Control, Launceston (the main station in Tasmania—not Hobart). The officer is in communcation with all staffed railway stations and logs train arrivals and departures and any delays.

Australian Railway Exploration Association (AREA) North–East tour train at Nabowla in March 1966. Pacifics M6 locomotive is on the left and an MA4 engine is on the right.

ABOVE At Lemana Junction, an X class and a car van on the main line, with a CCS hauling a few goods wagons waiting on the Mole Creek branch line to the left.

BELOW Engine MA 4 on an AREA train on their North–East Line excursion in March 1966. The photo is taken between Scottsdale and Ledgerwood and the train is travelling east.

ABOVE An M6 loco leaving Launceston with AREA Launceston –Nabowla excursion train in 1966.

RIGHT A 4-8-2 (wheel configuration) H5 locomotive on the electric-powered turntable at Devonport.

ABOVE An M6 locomotive taking water on the Burnie–Smithtown AREA excursion in March 1964.

ABOVE Leaving Launceston over the North Esk River Bridge with a mixed goods behind an MA class Pacific locomotive.

ABOVE The afternoon Delrane–Launceston local goods crossing the Bass Highway between Westbury and Hagley.

RIGHT At Smithton, a C12 locomotive is waiting with the goods for Redpa on the former Marrawah Tramway in December 1953. Note the wooden water tank.

ABOVE A C12 locomotive taking water at 18 Mile Tank on the Marrawah Tramway travelling to Redpa terminus.

RIGHT Another track level view of the train taking water at 18 Mile Tank in December 1955.

ABOVE Engine CCS 23 taking water at Mole Creek Station.

LEFT A CCS 2-6-0 locomotive with the Mole Creek to Deloraine goods in tow.

ABOVE An X class (X24) locomotive leaving Hobart Station and about to pass the Hobart Junction Signal Box.

RIGHT Interior of the Tasman Limited ACS articulated saloon carriage in 1955.

ABOVE Engine H5 at Western Junction with a centenary special in February 1971.

BELOW Engine CCS 23 and an MA Class locomotive with centenary special at Launceston in 1971.

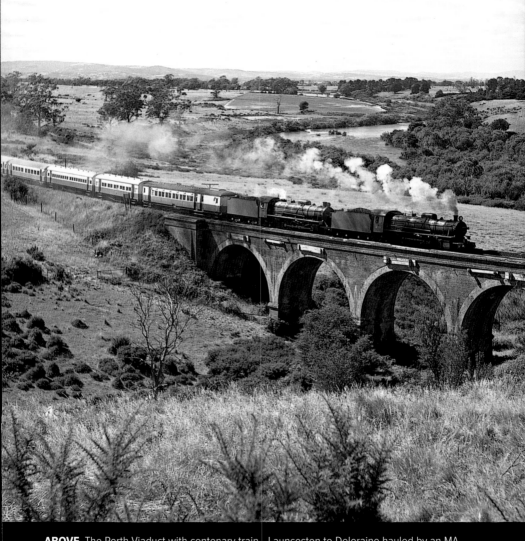

ABOVE The Perth Viaduct with centenary train—Launceston to Deloraine hauled by an MA locomotive and an H5 engine in February 1971. Note the former Sentinel-Cammell steam rail car behind the engines.

ABOVE Conara Junction from the St Marys train in December 1954. The stored Australian Standard Garratts represent two of six others placed out of service by the Tasmanian Government Railways.

RIGHT End of the Fingal branch line at St Marys. The passenger train from Conaroa Junction is being greeted by locals.

ABOVE Driver Bruce Jones (right), and his Irish fireman in the cab of M7 arrive late at Launceston.

BELOW Mixed train from Herrick on the North–East Line taking water at Karoola. Four of the ten M class Pacifics were rebuilt in 1957 and 1958 with four foot driving wheels replacing the four foot seven inch ones giving better traction on the North–East Line. These locomotives were classified as MA engines. This loco M7 was not rebuilt.

ABOVE An R class locomotive taking water.

RIGHT Emu Bay Railway—Australian Standard Garratt (ASG) southbound from Burnie taking water at Ridgley in the early morning. The Emu Bay Railway was a privately operated line.

A southbound ASG locomotive with goods after early departure from Burnie.

ABOVE The Burnie goods taking water at the thirty two and a half mile tank on the private Emu Bay railway. These Garratts were obtained secondhand from Queensland Government Railways and the Tasmanian Government Railways. The Emu Bay Railway was the only system to operate these engines successfully.

ABOVE The March 1964 AREA excursion train had a Tasman Limited articulated ACS saloon car. The loco is ASG 16.

203

ABOVE Engine ASG 16 on the AREA excursion at Zeehan in March 1964.

OPPOSITE PAGE
TOP An ASG with engine V9 on an adjacent track, in Zeehan Yard.

BOTTOM An Emu Bay Railway Dubs engine on a goods arriving at Zeehan from Burnie in December 1954. Two of these engines were converted to oil burning, semi streamlined and

ABOVE One of the Emu Bay Railway Dubs engines (number 8) converted to an oil burner and given a west coast name seen here on the *West Coaster* at Ridgely.

BELOW Leaving Ridgely.

ABOVE The *West Coaster* Zeehan-bound between Burnie and Ridgely. Note the Dial Range in the background.

BELOW The *West Coaster* between Zeehan and Guildford. Note the cars being carried as there was no through road at the time this photograph was taken.

ABOVE Locomotive Murchison at Guildford Junction. The branch to Waratah served the tin mines out at Mount Bishoff. The line was closed in 1940.

BELOW On the long-closed Waratah Branch, Emu Bay Railway number 4 locomotive, built by Martin.

PHOTO: UNKNOWN

RIGHT The Argent Tunnel on the Emu Bay Railway.

BELOW Emu Bay Railway Walker/Gardener 153 horsepower articulated diesel rail car, number WG 1, in service 1940, bogie trailer 2.

ABOVE Emu Bay Railway North British/Paxman Voith engine. It was a diesel-hydraulic, boasted 530 horsepower, had a 0-8-0 wheel configuration and was built in 1953.

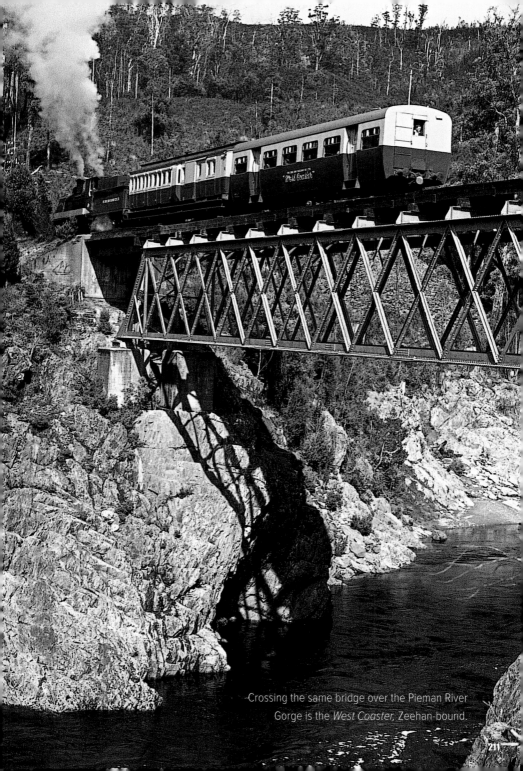

Crossing the same bridge over the Pieman River Gorge is the *West Coaster*, Zeehan-bound.

Image text on ticket: TULLAH ORE TREATMENT LIMITED / FARRELL JUNCTION / 935 .. TO · / TULLAH / FARE 2/9 / Issued by / 12/1 19 60 / THIS TICKET IS NOT / AVAILABLE UNTIL / SIGNED ON BACK

ABOVE On the U-curve not far from the junction.

OPPOSITE PAGE

TOP *Wee Georgie Wood* leaving interchange sidings with the Emu Bay Railway at Farrell Junction for the 5 mile (8 kilometre) journey to the isolated mining township of Tullah.

BOTTOM *Wee Georgie* at Farrell Junction with driver George Goodson and the fireman.

The first black tiger snake had been killed on the way to the junction. I was told these snakes always travelled in pairs. This is the second of the pair, despatched by the fire irons on the return journey.

ABOVE Taking water one and a half miles (2.4 kilometres) from Farrell Junction. *Wee Georgie Wood* carried silver and lead ore out and provisions and equipment in. People travelled the same way—or walked!

BELOW A load of firewood being pushed to Tullah.

ABOVE At Tullah, ready to depart on the 5 mile (8 kilometre) journey to the junction, which took around an hour. This trip was made twice a day.

OPPOSITE PAGE
TOP Crossing the Macintosh River in December 1954. When clear of the bridge, George's offsider ran back to the girders and placed a long tree branch across the track. I asked what that was for and was told it was to keep the cows in! Note the 44 gallon drums holding water in case *Wee Georgie* set fire to the bridge superstructure.

BOTTOM Driver George Goodson and *Wee Georgie* having arrived at Tullah.

ABOVE At West Strahan in December 1954, Tasmania Government Railways C class engine 2-6-0, after arriving from Zeehan, will soon move its short train to Strahan.

OPPOSITE PAGE

TOP At Tullah. Note the bracing on the wooden carriage that prevented it collapsing during the rough journeys!

BOTTOM *Wee Georgie* now fully restored and operating at Tullah.

ABOVE Mount Lyell Mining and Railway Company's Kraus 0-4-0 T number 10 (tank engine) at Queenstown working on 2 foot gauge track hauling a 3 foot six gauge wagon.

OPPOSITE PAGE

TOP Renovated Mount Lyell carriage at Regatta Point in 1954. This carriage is now operating on the Puffing Billy Line in Victoria.

BOTTOM At Strahan, two young ladies standing in a 4 wheel wagon to obtain the best possible views through the King River Gorge.

ABOVE The Iron Bridge over the King River at Teepookana.
PHOTO: DON STEPHENS

ABOVE Quarter Mile Bridge between Teepookana and Dubbil Barril crossing the King River.
PHOTO: DON STEPHENS

ABOVE Checking the rack engine and passenger carriage at Dubbil Barril.
PHOTO: DON STEPHENS

OPPOSITE PAGE
TOP At Dubbil Barril. Note the begining of the rack between the rails straight ahead, the beginning of the incline and ABT system.

BOTTOM The permanantly flushing toilet at Dubbil Barril.

ABOVE At Dubbil Barril, rack engine with homemade stock wagon.

ABOVE Engine standing on the rack section of the line.

PHOTO: DON STEPHENS

ABOVE Passing another train on the siding, not far out of Dubbil Barril. On the steep incline, either side of Rinadeena, a cog wheel under the engine driven by its own cylinders engaged in the rack centre rail seen here to prevent the adhesion driving wheels from slipping, and to assist in braking the trains on the downgrades.

PHOTO: DON STEPHENS

OPPOSITE PAGE *'Ambrose'* working on the rack to Rinadeena.

PHOTO: DON STEPHENS

ABOVE King River Gorge near the junction with the Queen River, which flows through Queenstown, as seen from the climbing train.

ABOVE The Ida Bay Railway, the most southerly railway in Australia, carried limestone from a quarry for onward passage to the Electrona Carbide Works. Technically there were a couple of small coal mining lines further south, but this is generally considered the most southerly line.

OPPOSITE PAGE On the Lake Margaret Tramway, which ran from the hydro town to the main road into Queenstown. This motor was known as *Vauxhall* and was dated 1938. It is assumed that this was when it was adapted for rail by the Mount Lyell Mining and Railway Company.

SOUTH AUSTRALIA

I n South Australia, financial and political difficulties, like those experienced in New South Wales and Victoria, had to be overcome before the first line was constructed. In 1847, Parliament passed the first legislation to open the way for railways in South Australia, and in 1850 Governor Henry Young began assessing the possibility of a railway line to and from the Murray River. The way was clouded in controversy, however, with a petition against a railway system even making its way to Queen Victoria in England, so the project was delayed.

Despite these early problems, steady progress was made from the 1850s until South Australia possessed a system adequate to fulfil the vital function of transporting passengers and primary industry alike. The railways were a major advancement in transporting people between the major and often isolated population hubs of South Australia.

A Horsedrawn Train

In early 1854 South Australia's first railway was a horsedrawn vehicle resembling a stagecoach that ran between Goolwa and Port Elliott. It became known as the Goolwa to Port Elliott Tramway. This railway/tramway had the distinction of being the first constructed for public convenience in all the mainland colonies that would one day federate to become Australia. Tasmania also had a convict-powered trolley that dated back to the 1830s.

Adelaide to Port Adelaide

It was another two years before South Australia saw its first loco-hauled train.This story began in 1850, when a private company proposed constructing a line between Adelaide and Port Adelaide (known as the Adelaide City and Port Railway). It connected a quarry in the city with the port. In 1851, with delays mounting, a five year plan was implemented, with the railway to be built as a broad gauge five foot three inch (1600mm) line.

This decision was made after Governor Young received confirmation from New South Wales that it too would build its railways as broad gauge, a decision later reversed and one that would have ramifications for more than 100 years.

Many disputes between the government and the private builder occurred during construction. After 18 months the line was abandoned by the Adelaide City and Port Railway Company—with no track laid. The government immediately took over the project, and finally on 19 April 1856 the first-loco hauled train ran in South Australia. It had cost £186,000 to build. For the first journey, 150 tickets were issued at one guinea each.

South Australia's first three locomotives were manufactured by Fairbairns in Manchester, and were named *Adelaide*, *Victoria* and *Albert*.

From Broken Hill to Oodnadatta

Expansion began with a line to Gawler opening in 1857, then over the next decade with lines and extensions to Kapunda and Burra.

All these early lines were constructed in broad gauge, but by the 1870s a number of isolated narrow gauge lines began to appear in South Australia. These three foot six lines pushed inland from Port Augusta and Port Pirie and other coastal ports into the hinterlands. By 1887 the narrow gauge line from Port Pirie had reached towns like Peterborough and Cockburn, a distance of more than 200 miles (321 kilometres). From Cockburn this narrow gauge line connected with the private Silverton Tramway, allowing lead, zinc and silver to be carried by rail from Broken Hill in New South Wales to the smelters at Port Pirie. The New South Wales government would not allow South Australia to build a line into New South Wales!

South Australian Railways spread to places like the Eyre Peninsula and Oodnadatta—later to be extended to Alice Springs by Commonwealth Railways —while the original Goolwa Tramway connected to Victor Harbor and Strathalbyn. Loco-hauled trains finally serviced the line in 1885.

BELOW The Adelaide Railway Station Concourse. This station used to serve interstate, intrastate and suburban trains, however, it now only serves the latter.

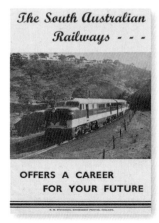

South Australian Railways spread to places like the Eyre Peninsula and Oodnadatta—later to be extended to Alice Springs by Commonwealth Railways —while the original Goolwa Tramway connected to Victor Harbor and Strathalbyn. Loco-hauled trains finally serviced the line in 1885.

SOUTH AUSTRALIAN RAILWAYS

Locomotives — Steam and Diesel Electric — and Rolling Stock

ABOVE Engine 747 backs onto its train in the platform at Adelaide Station. This shot was taken long before the platforms were covered for a commercial development.

PHOTO: JACK BABBAGE

Memories

Recently I wandered around Adelaide's National Railway Museum at Port Dock and was reunited with the South Australian Railways Cafeteria Car, which was on the consist of the **East West Express** connecting train with the **Trans-Australia Express**. The trains connected at Port Pirie. The car was very 'American' and streamlined in appearance.

I recall changing trains at Terowie on a Sunday night. It was the connecting train from Adelaide to Broken Hill—a connection that occurred as the rail gauges changed from broad to narrow. I became fascinated by the narrow gauge Y class engine at the platform; it was so small it was as if I was looking down on the boiler! Time came to board the train and I could not find a spare seat anywhere. Then I realised. Railways like this one were a vital link for inland Australian communities. After a weekend in Adelaide, workers were returning to Broken Hill so they could start work on Monday.

At Peterborough the train came to a stand and in a very short time I felt the bump of a 400 class Garratt coupling onto what had been the rear end, which now faced Broken Hill. As I could not find anywhere to sit, let alone sleep (over two seats) because of what some of the miners were doing, I was able to entertain myself with the roaring sounds of the Garratt's exhaust and the urgent shriek of its whistle.

I also recall travelling from Adelaide to Melbourne on **The Overland** when it departed from beautiful Adelaide Station. This stainless steel train was fitted with barn doors at the vestibules and while climbing through the Adelaide Hills it was such a thrill to view the spread of the carpet of lights below as **The Overland** curved away towards Mount Lofty.

On my earliest visit to South Australia I was amazed by the appearance of the South Australian steam locomotives with their modern American look. I later found that this American influence came from a commissioner, William Webb, who served for some time as president of a US railroad, and also a chief mechanical engineer, Frank Shea. Their influence in the 1920s shaped the unique look of South Australian Railways for years to come.

South Australia has the best representation of all railway gauges and is home to the most magnificent station building of them all in Adelaide.

ABOVE Engine number 500 leaving Adelaide station for Melbourne.

PHOTO: SAR

ABOVE A 500 class locomotive on the *Melbourne Express* (originally the *Intercolonial Express*). From 1936 this train was known as *The Overland*.

PHOTO: SAR

BELOW Engine number 500 converted to a 500 B, which indicated that a booster had been fitted in the trailing truck. At this time they were fitted a valance plate along the side with *The Overland* logo, painted dark green on it. The smoke box door was silver. The steam-powered booster provided assistance on the difficult climb through the Adelaide Hills.

PHOTO: SAR

ABOVE A 520 class locomotive with an excursion train out of Adelaide in March 1964.

RIGHT Engine 531 at Adelaide Station.

ABOVE The same excursion train near Ulooloo. Note the *Spirit of Progress* cars immediately behind the engine.

BELOW An excursion train with engine 522 in the 'down' platform at Gawler heading north out of Adelaide.

ABOVE Engine number 500 on an excursion train at Mount Barker.

PHOTO: JACK BABBAGE

BELOW Engine number 500, the last operating member of its class, seen on its last run.

RIGHT Engine number 700 at Adelaide Station on an enthusiasts train, which included some joint stock (VR-SAR) *Overland* cars.

BELOW The Victorian parlor car named *Yarra* on the end tail of the Australian Railway Enthusiasts Tour train, about to depart for Melbourne. Note the clerestory roof—typical of early rolling stock.

PARLOR CAR

ABOVE A 620 class engine (number 621) in October 1962 at Mount Lofty. Note the smoke deflectors on the engine.

BELOW A 620 class locomotive on a pasenger train at Ellen Street Station (located in the middle of the road), Port Pirie. Note that the five foot three inch (1600mm) gauge train is standing on dual gauge track. The three foot six inch (1067mm) gauge went to Peterborough and through to Broken Hill.

PHOTO: SAR

ABOVE Three foot six inch gauge train in Ellen Street at Port Pirie, 1966.

BELOW A 620 class locomotive (number 628) in steam at Mile End.

ABOVE Retired engine 504 at Mile End awaiting restoration as an exhibit in the National Railway Museum at Port Dock Adelaide. At the time the museum was only a dream, but it's now one of the leading railway museums in Australia.

BELOW A broad gauge locomotive (RX 230) taking water in Mile End Yard, Adelaide.

ABOVE Oil-fired locomotive T198 on a goods train waiting to depart for Peterborough.

BELOW A South Australian Railways (SAR) narrow gauge Beyer-Garratt number 406 at Peterborough. These locomotives were built under licence in France and were gauge convertible: from three foot six inches to
five foot three inches (1600mm) and four foot eight and a half inches (1435mm). Both T and 400 class engines were oil burners.

ABOVE T255 climbing Paratoo Bank.

PHOTO: JACK BABBAGE

LEFT Engine 409 making smoke, Belalie.

PHOTO: JACK BABBAGE

RIGHT A T class with short goods crossing the plain.

COMMONWEALTH RAILWAYS

Commonwealth Railways operated the Trans-Australian Railway, the Central Australia Railway and the North Australia Railway; important links that brought the states together and traversed some of Australia's most desolate terrain. These trains and long distance travel were embraced by the nation.

Across the Nullarbor

The building of the Trans-Australian Railway began with a sod turning ceremony at Port Augusta on 14 September 1912. Five months later another sod for the line was turned at Kalgoorlie. However, it was a time of political turmoil between Western Australia and the newly formed Commonwealth and it wasn't until 1917 that assent was given with the *Commonwealth Railways Act*.

On 14 October 1917, the lines were finally linked, allowing the first passenger train to depart from Port Augusta for Kalgoorlie eight days later, on a journey that would traverse 1051 miles (1691 kilometres).

Incredibly, for most of the journey there was no running water to be found, so bores and reservoirs were dug so the engines could take on water. Later engineers had to contend with the corrosive properties of this water, which caused havoc to the steam engines' boilers. A suitable treatment for the water was formulated several years later.

Ballasting of the line was not completed until 1940. You were probably in for a bumpy ride in those early years!

Passenger trains were hauled by G class locomotives, which were patterned on the New South Wales Government Railways' (NSWGR) 32 class engines, with the addition of larger carrying capacity tenders for the long distances. These engines were also required to haul goods trains because of the slow delivery of the 2-8-0 goods locomotives.

The C class engine also used this line after being introduced in 1938. These 4-6-0 locomotives were a virtual copy of the NSWGR 36 class.

Air-conditioned lounge and dining cars were introduced in February 1936. Showers made it into the carriages much earlier, first being introduced into the sleeping cars in March 1918.

Changing for Gauges

Up until the lage 1930s passengers heading to the eastern states had to alight at Port Augusta for the change of gauge. If they were coming from Perth this was the second change of trains; the first being at Kalgoorlie. From Port Augusta, South Australian passengers travelled through Quorn and Peterborough, on the narrow gauge, with a change again at Terowie. This would put them on the broad gauge for conveyance to Adelaide. There was another change (in latter years to *The Overland*), in Adelaide, though not because of the gauge.

People travelling on from Melbourne then took *Spirit of Progress* to Albury, changing again to standard gauge to complete the journey to Sydney.

A Standard Across Australia

On 26 July 1937 this very complicated journey was partially simplified by the construction of a standard gauge line from Port Augusta to Port Pirie Junction, one of the few places in the world where the main lines of three different gauges converged.

The first main line Clyde GM type diesel-electric locomotive (GM.1) was recieved at Port Augusta on 22 September 1951. By July 1962 this locomotive had run over 1, 500,000 miles (2,414,016 kilometres).

THE CLYDE-G.M. DIESEL ELECTRIC LOCOMOTIVE BUILT FOR THE COMMONWEALTH RAILWAYS

Two completely air-conditioned passenger trains manufactured by Wegmann & Co in Germany went into regular service in November 1952. a special feature was the observation/lounge/sleeping car with a rounded end, not unlike the parlor car of *Spirit of Progress*.

By early 1970 it was finally possible to travel from Sydney to Perth on the one standard gauge train. The train gained international acclaim as the stainless steel *Indian Pacific* (now privately owned by Great Southern Railways), which crossed the barren Nullarbor Plain. This line is most famous for the longest stretch of straight track in the world—a staggering distance of 300 miles (482 kilometres) without a curve.

The Central Australia Railway

After the introduction of the *Indian Pacific*, many of the Wegmann cars were transferred to the Central Australia Railway. They were given an exchange of bogies for the narrow three foot six inch (1067mm) gauge line that carried the *The Ghan*. While the air-conditioning made the journey much more comfortable in these newer cars, they also took away the charm and character of the original train to Alice Springs.

The Central Australia Railway included two famous sections: the Pichi Richi Pass and the line to Alice Springs that carried *The Ghan*. In the early years it was part of a grand vision to construct a main Northern Line all the way to Darwin.

North Australia Railway

From 4 September 1929 until the mid 1970s, Darwin had a railway station with an isolated section of track that extended down to Birdum in the Northern Territory as part of this dream. It was known as the North Australia Railway and part of it opened as early as 1888. Services were withdrawn in 1976 and the line was officially closed in 1981.

One section of the Main Northern Line (C.B. Anderson, Commisioner SAR called it this during South Australian Railways centenary celebrations) was through the Pichi Richi Pass, which opened on 15 December 1879; a section of railway that linked Port Augusta with Quorn. This rugged section of line became known for its steep grades and sharp curves. The line was closed to regular traffic in 1957 because of a standard gauge bypass, but today is operated by the Pichi Richi Railway Preservation Society. This line became part of Commonwealth Railways in 1911,
when control was transferred to the Federal Government.

Quorn became a hub of activity and later an important stop for the train to Alice Springs—*The Ghan*—which commenced service under that name in 1923. The *Great Northern Express* was renamed the *Afghan Express* from this date, after the cameleers who helped open up inland Australia with their 'ships of the desert'. These were mostly Indians from the north-west of the sub-continent (Pakistan from 1947) bordering Afghanistan. They came with their camels and settled wherever they were needed. The strings of camels carried loads of sleepers and fixings, food and water. The Indians also serviced outlying properties from Marree to south-west Queensland. They became incorrectly known as Afghans which, in Australian fashion, was shortened to 'Ghans'. Relatively few were actually from Afghanistan.

The railway was extended to Oodnadatta in 1891 by the SAR, then Commonwealth Railways reached Alice Springs with a three foot six inch gauge from Oodnadatta through Marree. The narrow gauge line from Quorn became
a link between Perth and Adelaide for trans-Australia passengers and goods.

Memories

In 1959 I travelled from Port Augusta to Alice Springs and return. The line was standard gauge from Port Augusta to Marree, where it was necessary to change trains to the old **Ghan**, which departed from Marree after 10pm. The train travelled through the night, making just enough stops to keep one awake. Daylight, and relief, came when the train arrived at Edward's Creek. After leaving Edward's Creek with the sun rising in the east I began to wonder how I'd slept on the uncomfortable second class seat (all my Holiday Pass would allow). Perhaps it was the gentle swaying of the very slow moving carriage and the muted, rhythmic clack of the wheels on rail joints.

Three hours and 64 miles (102 kilometres) later, we were approaching Oodnadatta; the largest 'dot' on the map between Marree and Alice Springs. Here I discovered that **The Ghan** consisted of 14 bogie freight cars next to the two diesel-electric Sulzer locomotives, followed by nine passenger cars including the sleepers, a dining car and a van—and the train was only 40 minutes late! **The Ghan** stopped with the last car opposite the corrugated iron pub and there was a mass exodus of men, who made for the oasis entrance. They were swallowed by the building in one gulp. All was quiet and despite the train running quite late, the stop seemed longer than at any other settlement. I began to think that there was some agreement between the driver, guard and publican! Then, suddenly, there was a jolt and **The Ghan** crept forward. As the van passed the pub there were a number of distant horn blasts from the lead engine set off by the driver. Men stampeded through the front door, their thirst only partially satisfied. Did they run to jump on the nearest moving carriage? No! They kept racing, some stumbling, to reach the cars where they thought their seats were. Another blast from the distant horn, a touch on the throttle to increase acceleration and anxiety ... The stragglers leapt on the nearest passing steps. After all, the next train to the Alice was not for three days! I left Alice Springs on the next southbound **Ghan** after only one day of sightseeing.

During the stop at Finke I counted 30 bogie freight cars, nine passenger cars including the diner and two vans. A long train. The freight cars were marshalled behind the pair of Sulzer diesel-electric engines and the passenger cars behind them. To ensure a rough ride, I surmised. And I was to find out I was correct! Here I noticed an ageing Aboriginal man sauntering towards the dining car from a dry creek bed shaded by peppercorn trees; his family camp. He stopped and looked up at an open window through which one of the cooks leaned. The cook then disappeared for a moment, returning with a large cut-glass bowl of green jelly!

The Aborigine looked at the cook, smiled and nodded his thanks then returned to his family. I suppose the bowl was returned to the next Alice-bound **Ghan**!

Having crossed the dry Finke River (claimed to be the oldest in the world), the train wandered along until it reached Pedirka, just over three hours and 85 miles (136 kilometres) from Finke. It was here that a 'hot box' was found on an axle bearing. How was this possible on a train travelling at not much more than walking pace! By the time this flat-top was shunted into a siding, the **Ghan** was getting later. I watched a beautiful orange sunset as we neared Oodnadatta (no pub stop; this time dinner was being served). While waiting for my meal I observed a beautiful full moon rising from below the eastern horizon, burning its way through the low haze of orange dust.

Later, riding on the end platform of a carriage to view the desert by moonlight on either side of the line, I felt that I may have worked out why the passenger cars were at the end of the train. We were in sand dune desert—drifting sand— and the line was built over the hills, not through them in a cutting as in more stable terrain. If the line had passed through cuttings every time there was a windstorm the rails would have been buried, possibly even causing a derailment at night.

Now, this **Ghan** was long and heavy. When descending a hill the driver allowed all 41 vehicles to bunch up on his engines with a clanking of all the 'Chopper' couplings, which were built with some slack. He began the climb of the next hill cautiously then suddenly opened the throttle wide to charge and challenge the next sand hill. There was clanking and banging as the slack in the couplings of the freight cars took up—almost frightening in its savagery. Then it was the turn of the passenger cars and what a shock for anyone aleep or near so! By now the twin locos were well up the sandhill, exhausts roaring. Only when all the coupling slack was taken up did the diesels begin to slow. The dune was beaten by man and his machines. Over the summit and down the other side. **The Ghan** was drawn over the top and was ready for the next dune.

The first (GM1) General Motors Electro Motive Division locomotive at Clyde Engineering Company, Granville, NSW, in the works yard on its presentation to Commonwealth Railways. It was received at Port Augusta on 22 September 1957 and by July 1962 it had completed 1,500,000 miles (2,414,016 kilometres).

ABOVE Engine G1, the first engine to haul a passenger train across the Nullarbor from Port Augusta to Kalgoorlie. It has been restored and is exhibited in the National Railway Museum, Port Dock, Adelaide.

RIGHT The remains of one of the original G class locomotives, which copied the NSWGR 32 class.

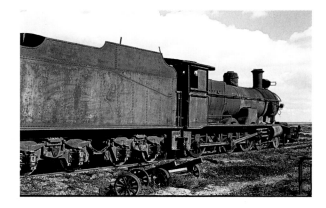

ABOVE To commemorate Captain James Cook's landing in Australia in 1770, the NSW Rail Transport Museum organised a journey from Sydney to Perth and Leightonfield marshalling yard 200 years later in 1970. It is seen here at Cook on the Nullarbor Plain—the longest straight stretch of railway in the world. Contrary to popular opinion, this stop is actually named after Sir Joseph Cook a former prime minister. With engine 3801 at the head, she became the first and only steam locomotive to travel from Sydney to Perth and return on a passenger train.

BELOW At another stop on the Nullarbor, Clyde-built GM Locomotive re-engined and now classified as CL3 is about to detach from the train and run forward for photographic purposes

ABOVE On the scrap road at Port Augusta are, on the left, two C class 4-6-0 locomotives, modelled on the NSWGR 36 class engines; and on the right two L class locos built by Clyde Engineering for export to China. They never made it to China and weren't needed by Commonwealth Railways.

ABOVE A freight train crossing the Nullarbor, hauled by three
diesel-electric locomotives. Note the crew car coupled to the locomotives.

ABOVE An excursion train arriving at the narrow gauge Central Australian Railway Station at Hawker. This station was on the original line from Port Augusta to Alice Springs.

BELOW The abandoned Beltana station, station-master's residence and goods shed on the former narrow gauge line.

ABOVE An NM class engine of the CAR (Commonwealth Australian Railway) descending Pichi Richi Pass towards Port Augusta. Note how the spans of the bridge have been reinforced between the original piers with the advent of double heading engines and heavier loads.

BELOW An NM locomotive climbing through Pichi Richi Pass to Quorn, below the Devil's Peak near Saltia Bridge in April 1964.

ABOVE At the change of gauge station, Marree, locomotive NM 25 on an excursion train at the three foot six inch gauge platform waits for the arrival of a standard gauge train from Port Augusta. The NMs were copies of the Queensland Railway C17 class, the most numerous narrow gauge steam engines in Australia

BELOW The train passes a rail bridge destroyed by a derailment. It is crossing over a dry river bed.

ABOVE Two Sulzer diesel-electric locomotives on a southbound *Ghan* at Pedirka, late winter 1959. Approaching Pedirka the engine crew had noticed thin grey smoke rising from underneath the flat car just ahead of the passenger cars.

ABOVE The owner of the motor car would have been a little upset when told where his car was! This was the flat car with the hot box that had to be shunted into a siding for attention and then forwarding by the next train south. Note the louvres on the first carriage to help shade the passengers in the summer. The car that is wider and higher than all the others is the dining car originally operated on the Trans-Australian Railway standard gauge line across the Nullarbor. None of these cars is air-conditioned.

ABOVE The Sentinel steam railcar at Darwin Railway Station in the earlier part of the 20th century. This passenger service was known to locals as 'Leaping Lena' because of the rough ride.

BELOW Early traffic on the original narrow gauge railway south of Darwin.

ABOVE Parliamentary party visit in 1912.

PHOTO: FEDERAL PARLIAMENTARY PARTY VISIT 1912, NORTHERN TERRITORY LIBRARY

After an absence of more than a quarter of a century, trains returned to Darwin in 2004. Today *The Ghan* continues through Alice Springs to Darwin, while the new railway also opens up freight routes from Adelaide and all states. Here *The Ghan* is photographed at the new Darwin Railway Station.

PHOTO: GREAT SOUTHERN RAILWAY LTD

FROM RAILWAYS TO TRAMWAYS

T he development of light rail has seen the resurgence of tramway traffic on former rail corridors.

South Australia

In South Australia, the railway from the Adelaide beachside suburb of Glenelg was connected to the city in 1873. It was a private line operated by steam trains. In 1881, the Glenelg Railway Company, having purchased two other private railways operating along the route, began services operating from the beach to North Terrace. The South Australian Government took control of this line in 1899. By 1929 the line had been converted to a standard gauge electric line over the same route and operated by electric trams, resembling US inter-urban cars. These H class cars operated in regular service until 2007—an incredible feat. A service using these cars still runs on weekends and these are known as the 'Heritage Trams'.

The H cars originally had trolley poles connecting the tram to the overhead wire, but in later years these were replaced by 'bow-collectors' (like a pantograph), which are not prone to de-wirements. The H cars were replaced by 'light rail vehicles' and the service was extended

back through King William Street (the city centre), from where they had been removed half a century before. This reconstructed line continues on, turning left into North Terrace, with a stop at Adelaide Railway station, then on to terminate opposite a campus of Adelaide University. There are plans to extend the line even further.

Victoria

Melbourne has two light rail lines. The first from opposite Station Pier (Port Melbourne), follows the route of Australia's first steam railway to Melbourne. However, the track gauge is now four foot eight and a half inches so the light rail vehicles can enter the Melbourne street tramway system, now one of the largest in the world. This light rail line can trace its origins to 1854.

Although it was originally a steam line, it became part of the Melbourne Electric railway system, at which time the line was truncated opposite Station Pier.

The other light rail line runs from St Kilda and enters the former railway reservation giving passengers a fast and unobstructed ride into the city. Along the line old station buildings are clearly visible and are well maintained. This line joins the other light railway to Station Pier, continuing into the city and beyond. Like the Station Pier line, this line can trace its origins to the earliest days of railways in Victoria, having originally opened in 1857.

New South Wales

Sydney too has introduced a successful, privately owned and operated light railway that uses former rail corridors. Originally opened in August 1997 and since extended, the line uses part of the rail extension to Darling Harbour, which dates back to 1857. Today the line runs through to the Inner West, reaching Catherine Street, Lilyfield by riding on the formations of the old Darling Harbour Goods railway line, which was built to alleviate congestion on the passenger lines around Sydney.

At the city end, the line runs beside the Sydney Markets, crossing George Street, running along Hay Street and up to Sydney Terminal Station along the former tram corridor—only this time in reverse to the old tramway system that closed operations to the collonade in 1957.

The line provides an interesting ride, with a long viaduct at Wentworth Park, deep cuttings and even tunnels. This former railway section dates back to the 1920s.

Today, governments are being forced to look at progressive and alternate transport options for cities, and light rail is proving to be viable, efficient and reliable. In an about turn, major cities around the world are going back to the past, utilising old rail and tram corridors for light rail operations, and developing new systems.

ABOVE Victoria Square-bound in Adelaide, a coupled set of H cars on the Glenelg tramway.

BELOW At the then Victoria Square Terminus these cars resembled US Inter-Urban or Pacific Electric vehicles. They were built in 1929 for the converted steam to electric line, originally a service operated from the beachside suburb of Glenelg through Adelaide CBD. Early photographs show that up to three cars coupled were in operation. Originially the electric vehicles ran onto the street tramway line to North Terrace where they terminated at Adelaide Railway Station.

ABOVE The 1929-built H cars ran until 2007, when they were replaced by the new German-built 'Bombardier' Flexity light rail vehicles, seen here in King William Street, Adelaide.

BELOW A Glenelg-bound vehicle on the line which has been diverted around the Western border of Victoria Square. Note that the grass between and beside the rails is artificial!

ABOVE An air-conditioned Flexity light rail vehicle shown here passing through the CBD in King William Street. It will turn into North Terrace, pass Adelaide Railway Station and terminate opposite a campus of Adelaide University. This extension from Victoria Square was opened in 2007.

BELOW Two light rail vehicles in Sydney in Hay Street. The right-hand vehicle is leaving the ramp from the colonnade of Sydney Terminal Station, which formerly carried street trams from Circular Quay via Pitt Street. These trams work their way through to Lilyfield on the former goods railway lines and have proven very successful.

PHOTO: IAN DODD

ABOVE A light rail vehicle, heading towards and through Melbourne aproaching the Albert Park Stop. The vehicle will continue on through the city centre to East Brunswick. Note that the light rail platform is at footpath level. The orginal railway buildings remain but are out of use.

RIGHT Another Flexity light rail vehicle approaching the junction with the St Kilda line. This vehicle had left Port Melbourne on the former railway reservation and will travel through the city to Mont Albert

TRAIN TRAVEL...
THEN AND NOW

Early passenger carriages were carried on just four wheels. Later came six-wheel radial trucks, followed by four-wheeled bogies, then six-wheeled bogies. Six-wheeled bogies carried the heavier steel frame, wooden sleeping cars and gave the most comfortable ride in the heavier sitting cars.

At the dawn of Australian railways, many systems had three classes of passenger travel, offering different levels of comfort and different fares. Often third class was little more than a timber cross bench in a windowless carriage, while first class offered curtains, padded seats and other trappings. This was later simplified to first class and economy for the most part. In later years, the difference between economy and first class blurred somewhat, usually the only differences being leg room and a different colour scheme!

More unfortunate travellers may have been condemned to ride in a 'dog box' side loading sitting car. Some of these cars date from the late 19th century, and one carriageworks even had a young Henry Lawson working on their construction!

Following the introduction of the luxurious, stainless steel all-sleeper train *Southern Aurora* in 1962, which ran between Sydney and Melbourne on the (finally completed) standard gauge line, came the *Indian Pacific*, which ran across the continent between east and west from February 1970.

This was followed by *The Alice*, which ran between Sydney and Alice Springs—leaving Sydney on Monday afternoons, with

a connection at Port Pirie in South Australia for Adelaide. Then there was the *Ghan*, which left Adelaide at 11am on Thursdays for Alice Springs, and the Trans-Australian, which left Adelaide on Wednesdays and Saturdays for Perth.

All of these were luxury air-conditioned trains with sleeping cars, restaurant and lounge cars.

These trains, except the *Southern Aurora*, were operated by Australian National Railways and staffed by an all male crew.

Sadly, due to operating losses, these train services were reduced and finally the luxury trains were tendered to the private sector.

Great Southern Railway purchased the operation, including the *Overland* between Adelaide and Melbourne. It now operates the *Ghan* between Adelaide, through The Alice to Darwin, and the refurbished *Overland* between Adelaide and Melbourne as a day train. It also operates the *Indian Pacific* between Sydney and Perth. Luxury train travel in Australia lives on in these great and internationally acclaimed routes.

ABOVE Interiors of lounge cars used on both the *Indian Pacific* and *The Ghan*.

Memories

*When I travelled to Melbourne on the **Melbourne Express** in a TAM 12-wheel sleeping car, probably built in the 1930s, it was good to stretch out on the berth. The six-wheeled bogie almost beneath the cabin beat out a pleasant and different rhythm and, once over the top of a grade, the carriage would gently rock from side to side and the tempo would gently increase. I had fitted a wooden framed, fine-screened soot eliminator on the window sill and closed the window down on it. This was designed to allow some air in to ventilate the cabin; however, in the morning I found it had very effectively acted as a sieve and fine black soot was distributed over much of the compartment.*

ABOVE A side loading economy (2nd) class sitting car. This carriage was built in August 1913 and withdrawn in October 1969. The compartment seated eight passengers (six in first class) and the unfortunate traveller who had the only remaining lifting seat to occupy was interrupted by all of the other seven passengers requiring to use the toilet. These carriages were used on both day trains and long distance trains, such as mail trains, which travelled all night through NSW.

PHOTO: SEAN POWE

LEFT Looking through to the WC. This car is in the NSW Rail Transport Museum, Thilmere.

PHOTO: SEAN POWE

RIGHT Sleeper cabin in 12-wheeled carriage EAM 1827 built in 1913 and withdrawn in 1978. Now operated by NSW Rail Transport Museum.

PHOTO: SEAN POWE

BELOW The folding wash basin in the sleeping compartment, which provided cold water only. Note the decorative art noveau inspired design on the pressed metal.

PHOTO: SEAN POWE

ABOVE A former Commonwealth Railways Trans-Australian Railway dining car now in the National Railway Museum Adelaide. Air-conditioned dining and lounge cars were introduced in 1936.

BELOW The interior of the 12-wheel dining car named *Adelaide* made by the Pullman Car Company in the USA. It could seat 48 people, and was used on *The Overland* until withdrawn in 1970. This car and the heavy Pullman sleeping car created a heavy load in the Adelaide Hills.

ABOVE The dining car of *Spirit of Progress*, which went into service between Albury and Melbourne in 1937.

BELOW The crew of a buffet dining car on a NSW railways air-conditioned *Daylight Express*.

ABOVE It's Christmas! In a NSW dining car on the Sydney–Melbourne *Daylight* the crew provided their own decorations and costumes as befitted the festive season.

LEFT The dining car crew pose for a photo.

OPPOSITE PAGE
TOP At the platform at Broken Hill, one of the many hotels in Argent Street is reflected in a window of the *Indian Pacific*, operated by Great Southern Railways Ltd. Great Southern Railway has two classes of travel: Gold Kangaroo Service and Red Kangaroo Service. Gold Kangaroo service offers travellers private suites with meals included, while Red Kangaroo is a regular passenger carriage.

BOTTOM In Red Kangaroo Service an example of day/nighter seats that provide the most economical travel on the longest distance rail journeys in Australia between destinations such as Perth, Adelaide, Darwin and Sydney. Meals are additional and collected in the buffet car.

ABOVE The Gold Service sleeping cabin for two, which is complete with an ensuite, is shown made up for day use. To convert to night use (into beds), the back of the seat pulls down revealing the bed. The top berth is also lowered to create a bed.

LEFT The lower berth bed made up for night use, complete with a toiletry bag.

ABOVE The Queen Adelaide Restaurant car used on the *Indian Pacific* and *The Ghan*.

RIGHT A table being set by one of the train staff in The Queen Adelaide Restaurant Car.

Jim Powe

10th August 1934 – 20th January 2009.

About the Author

Jim Powe's fascination with trains and trams began at the tender age of four. Once he could afford a camera, he avidly photographed Sydney's trams, which were fast disappearing. He decided he should also be shooting movies of these moving objects and this thought eventually led to Jim becoming a cinematographer. He worked in television and he concentrated on filming
steam trains in Australia and New Zealand in his spare time.

Jim realised that the captivating sounds of steam locomotives should be preserved and he has released a number of recordings, both of steam trains passing by and riding on them. He became a self-taught film editor and sound recordist.

Jim's videos include the Platinum Award winning and best selling 3801: A Legend in Steam, Moss Vale Train (available on DVD), In Steam (available on DVD), Films from the Archives, and Memories.

Jim's photographs are considered an extremely important archive of railway history in Australia and are sought after by museums and libraries alike. Most of the photographs in this book have never been published before.

Acknowledgements

I would like to thank the following people and organisations for helping collate and check the accuracy of content in this book and for access to collections.

Dennis O'Brien (NSW), Dr Jim Stokes (Tasmania), Ian Dodd, Jeff Austin (WA); Phil Melling (WA), Rod Milne (WA); Jack Babbage (SA), Kym Kalleske (SA), Australian Railway Historical Society (NSW), Australian Railway Historical Society (WA); NSW Rail Transport Museum, Great Southern Railways Ltd, National Railway Museum Adelaide; Rail Tram and Bus Union NSW, Peter O'Connor (*On Wooden Rails*), Balley Hooley Steam Railway, Port Douglas (Qld)

Thank you to New Holland Publishers' Managing Director, Fiona Schultz and her staff without whose assistance and talent this book would not have been created for those interested in Australian railways.

A special thank you to Linda Sarre. Her patience and ability to find items that I had given up on helped make this book possible.

Photo Credits

First published in Australia in 2008 by
This edition published in 2022
New Holland Publishers
Sydney

newhollandpublishers.com.au

Level 1, 178 Fox Valley Road, Wahroonga NSW 2076

A record of this book is held at the National Library of Australia.

ISBN 9781760795443

Publisher: Fiona Schultz
Designer: Ben Taylor (Taylor Design)
Editor: Jenny Scepanovic
Production Manager: Arlene Gippert
Printed in China